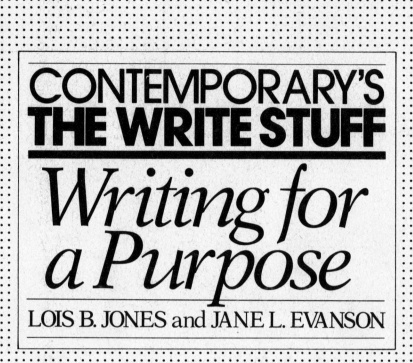

CONTEMPORARY'S
THE WRITE STUFF
Writing for a Purpose

LOIS B. JONES and JANE L. EVANSON

Consultant
Joyce A. Duffy
Austin Career Education Center
Chicago, Illinois

Project Editor
Ellen Carley Frechette

Editorial Director
Caren Van Slyke

CONTEMPORARY
BOOKS, INC.
CHICAGO

Library of Congress Cataloging-in-Publication Data

Jones, Lois B.
  The write stuff, writing for a purpose.

  1. English language—Rhetoric.   I. Evanson, Jane L.
II. Title.
PE1408.J834   1985   808'.042   85-10949
ISBN 0-8092-5453-0

Published by Contemporary Books, Inc.
180 North Michigan Avenue, Chicago, Illinois 60601
Manufactured in the United States of America
International Standard Book Number: 0-8092-5453-0

Published simultaneously in Canada by
Beaverbooks, Ltd.
195 Allstate Parkway
Valleywood Business Park
Markham, Ontario L3R 4T8
Canada

Editorial
Karin Evans
Christine M. Benton

Production Editor
Patricia Reid

Art and Illustrations
Princess Louise El
Ophelia M. Chambliss-Jones
Arvid Carlson
Frank Noto

Typography
Terrence Alan Stone

Design
Deborah Rank Popely

Cover Design
Robb Pawlak

Table of Contents

Notes to the Instructor

Adults have a wide variety of writing needs. Whether they are writing to a child's teacher or to a personnel manager, they need to approach the process without apprehension. Many people are reluctant to even get started writing because they know they will make mistakes in grammar and spelling. *Writing for a Purpose* will help students overcome this reluctance.

In this book, the real writing needs of adults are taught in a step-by-step process. Before actual writing begins, prewriting activities such as brainstorming and outlining are introduced. The book then proceeds through all stages of the writing process, ending with editing. The student should be encouraged to take one step at a time and not be preoccupied with correct grammar and spelling. Let the student know that there will be plenty of time later to go back and fix up his work.

Although *Writing for a Purpose* emphasizes the longer piece of writing, the student is given frequent opportunities to review the single paragraph, in the form of Paragraph Highlights. You should urge students to use these Highlights as they go through each chapter. These exercises serve as excellent refresher courses in the basic concepts of the paragraph.

By breaking down writing purposes into the four basic types of writing—narrative, descriptive, persuasive, and informative—the authors of *Writing for a Purpose* are able to give special hints and guidelines for specific writing tasks. Emphasis is placed on the real writing needs of adults—for essay tests, personal needs, and business communication. By the time your students complete the book, they will have developed both proficiency as writers and confidence in their writing ability.

1. Getting Ready to Write

The Longer Piece of Writing

In this book, we will work with pieces of writing that are more than one paragraph long. For many purposes, a topic may be too long to cover in just one paragraph. As a writer, you may not feel you can get your point across in one paragraph. In this book, you will learn the special organization and skills needed to write a longer piece.

Paragraphs: Parts of the Whole

There is a saying that the whole is only as good as the sum of its parts. Essays, business letters, and short stories are all made up of paragraphs. Therefore, to come up with a good longer piece of writing, you must write good paragraphs. Throughout this book, you will find reminders, hints, and exercises to help you improve your paragraphs. These hints are called **Paragraph Highlights**. They can serve as good checks for strengthening your work.

What's Your Purpose?

Before you begin putting anything on paper, make sure your purpose for writing is clear to you. Do you want to write to your child's teacher to set up an appointment? Do you have to write a memo to your job supervisor? Are you writing a letter to a friend or relative? Maybe you are writing an essay for a test. Even writing just to get your thoughts down is a purpose. Knowing your purpose will help you get started and keep you on track.

Depending on what your purpose is, you will use different kinds of paragraphs in your writing. You may use *narrative* paragraphs (to tell a story), *descriptive* (to describe someone or something), *informative* (to explain something), or *persuasive* (to give your point of view). Any piece of writing should fit into one of these basic categories. Knowing your purpose will help you decide which of these categories your writing falls into, and this will help you as you begin to write.

The exercise below will allow you to practice deciding on purpose. The examples are only one paragraph long, but you should picture them as parts of a longer piece of writing.

Exercise A: Know Your Purpose

 Read each short paragraph. In the first blank after each one, write *narrative* if the paragraph is telling a story, *descriptive* if it is describing someone or something, *informative* if it is explaining something, or *persuasive* if it gives a point of view. In the second blank, summarize the writer's purpose. The first one has been done for you.

EXAMPLE: To get to the GED testing site, turn left on Parker Road. Go three miles to the first large intersection and turn left again on Wingback Pike. The address is 6543 Wingback, and the building is on the right just past a supermarket.

informative

The writer's purpose is to *tell how to get to the GED testing site*

1. I really believe that every person should get involved in some kind of volunteer activity. Even once a week would be helpful to both the volunteer and the people she helps. If each citizen pitched in a little time, the world might be a better place.

_____

The writer's purpose is to _____

2. It's important for adults working with young teenagers to realize how prevalent drugs, sex, and alcohol are in the lives of these kids. We won't be able to reach them if we pretend these issues don't exist.

   _____

   The writer's purpose is to _____

   _____

3. When I answered the phone, a muffled voice asked me if I had seen my cat that day. I said no. The voice said, "What happened to your cat will happen to you if you don't—" and then suddenly the line went dead.

   _____

   The writer's purpose is to _____

   _____

4. The park is closed because of a health hazard. Due to a broken sewer line, sewage is seeping through the grass and presents a risk to those who may frequent the spot. Authorities say they expect to solve the problem by the weekend.

   _____

   The writer's purpose is to _____

   _____

5. When I left work yesterday, I didn't have any money, so I headed for home on foot. I walked through downtown, across the river, through the park, and up Clark Street. Forty blocks and two hours later, I finally opened my front door.

   _____

   The writer's purpose is to _____

   _____

6. You should have seen her face. She had jam on her chin, egg under one eye, and bacon grease smeared across her forehead. She was grinning from ear to ear, though.

   _____

   The writer's purpose is to _____

   _____

Continued

7. Treatment of cancer is much easier for patients now than it was five years ago. For example, modern radiation treatment doesn't make the patient nauseous.

—————————

The writer's purpose is to ———————————————————

————————————————————————————————————

THE ANSWERS CAN BE FOUND ON PAGE 11.

What's Your Topic?

Just as you need a topic to write a good paragraph, you also need to define your topic for a longer piece of writing. In most cases, you already have a purpose for writing and your topic is dependent on that purpose. For example, if you have to write a letter to apply for a job, you know that your topic is something like "my interest in working for this company." If you find you must give some directions to the baby-sitter or repairman, you do not need to sit down and choose a topic. In short, when you are writing for a specific purpose, your topic has already been decided.

However, you should not take this topic for granted. Be sure to have your topic clear in your mind before you begin to write. If you are writing a business letter, try to pinpoint what the overall topic of the letter will be. The clearer your topic is to you, the less your writing will stray into unrelated areas. Many writers find it helpful to jot their topics down instead of just keeping them in their heads. You may want to do this so that you will have something to refer to as you begin the writing process.

To Whom Are You Writing?

The answer to this question is important for two reasons. First of all, you will want to be careful of your choice of words as you write. Depending on whom you're writing to, you will choose either a more formal or a more conversational language. If you keep your audience in mind as you write, you can avoid having to go back and rewrite.

Keeping your audience in mind is important for another reason. It will affect what form your piece of writing will finally take. For example, your final version of a note to a friend about your new promotion will look very different from the business memo you write to your supervisor accepting the promotion. You will use different greetings and closings, and probably different paper. In short, your audience, or reader, should have a big effect on how you write and present yourself.

In this book, we will look at three types of writing: essays (as in a classroom setting or a writing test), business correspondence (as in job memos and letters), and personal (less formal) writing. This will help you to keep your reader in mind at all times.

PARAGRAPH HIGHLIGHT #1

In this Highlight, we will review the basic parts of a well-written paragraph:

- **the topic sentence**
- **the supporting sentences**
- **the concluding sentence (optional)**

The model paragraph below has these three important parts. See if you can point them out.

I would like to make an appointment with you to discuss my son, Allen Stone. He is in your seventh grade social studies class, and I realize he is having trouble. He complains about not seeing the blackboard and about frequent disruptions in the classroom. Although I work during the day, I can make special arrangements to meet with you. Please call me at 475-3000 anytime after 5:00 to set up an appointment. Thank you for your time in setting this up, Ms. Stenerude.

Sincerely,

Ronald Stone

The topic sentence, in dark type in the paragraph, introduces the topic and tells the reader what the paragraph will be about. The supporting sentences that follow all relate to the topic sentence and give you more information about the topic. The writer states in the topic sentence that he would like an appointment. The supporting sentences explain why he wants one and how he could arrange one. Finally, in the last or concluding statement, the writer thanks the reader and once again emphasizes his purpose in writing—to set up an appointment.

Paragraph Highlight Exercise 1

In Part 1 below, you will find three topic sentences. After each topic sentence, write two supporting sentences (and a concluding statement if you want) to complete each paragraph. Use the hints from the Highlight to help you.

In Part 2, you will find three paragraphs that do not have topic sentences. Read each through carefully, then write a topic sentence that summarizes the main idea of the paragraphs.

Part 1

1. As young people in this community, we should be given a place where we can meet and talk with other teenagers.

   _____

   _____

   _____

   _____

2. It's best to approach a new love relationship with caution.

   _____

   _____

   _____

   _____

3. I didn't finish high school because I didn't like it enough to stay.

   _____

   _____

   _____

   _____

Part 2

1. _____

   _____

   My older sister had to leave school to go to work when she was twelve. My older brother worked after school every day until ten o'clock, and then he would do his homework. Those were hard times.

2. _____

    _____

It has four-wheel drive, standard transmission, and a rugged body. Options are AM/FM stereo radio, carpeting, and air conditioning. It comes in mauve, lime, cinnamon, and silver.

3. _____

    _____

My English teacher's husband lives in North Carolina, over a thousand miles away. One of my co-workers drives four hours out to the country every weekend to where his wife lives. It's amazing that these marriages survive.

SOME POSSIBLE ANSWERS FOR THIS EXERCISE ARE ON PAGE 11.

Writing as a Process

There is one other important point to make before you begin to write. You will find that writing longer pieces is presented in a step-by-step approach in this book. You should look at your writing as just that—a step-by-step process. Don't be afraid that every word you put onto paper will be final. You will actually have several opportunities to change what you write. Remember that most writing that you see in books and newspapers has been changed and rewritten several times before anyone even looks at it.

Keep this in mind as you begin writing. Grammar and punctuation are important, as are word choice and sentence structure. But you can't worry about these things before you even have anything on paper! What you, the writer, have to say is the most important part of the writing process. Don't let anything get in your way.

Why More than One Paragraph?

When a writer tries to confine his thoughts to one paragraph, one of three things will happen. One is that it will work. Sometimes one paragraph is the right format and length for one's ideas. Pieces of writing such as a note to the paperboy, a short thank you letter, and a memo to your co-worker may need only one paragraph to get a point across. It all depends on how much you need to say.

In other cases, one paragraph is not enough space to make your point. If a writer tries to say too much in too little space, he either will come up with a very long paragraph or will shortchange the reader by leaving out important information. Look at how two different writers tried to fit what they had to say into one paragraph:

> I'm all for raising the prices for our parking lot for a couple of different reasons. First of all, drivers should share in paying the huge city tax our business now has to pay. Secondly, people who drive to work should have to pay for the convenience our new location is giving them.

In this paragraph, the writer has given us her ideas, but they are not well developed. We sense that she has a lot to say about the topic, but she doesn't give the reader enough information to convince him of her point of view. In short, she left out some good ideas so that she would need only one paragraph.

Now look at the paragraph below and decide if it is well written.

> I'm all for raising the prices for our parking lot for a couple of different reasons. Since we have proposed the increase, we have received a lot of complaints. But if our customers knew the reasons for the proposed hike, maybe they wouldn't be so down on it. First of all, drivers should share in paying the huge city tax our business now has to pay. We own a pretty big block of land, and we are taxed heavily for it. This money goes for city improvements that help drivers as well as the lot owners. Therefore, drivers should pay for part of this tax. Secondly, these drivers should have to pay for the added convenience of our new location. Why should they expect to pay the same amount for a space three blocks from work as they have always paid for a space seven blocks away? Better service always calls for higher prices, in my opinion.

This writer has all the right ideas here, and he has developed these thoughts well. However, did you notice how tiresome it got to read such a long group of sentences? The ideas all start running together, and it is easy to forget the writer's purpose and point of view.

No matter how you look at it, the one-paragraph format is not effective in covering this topic. A logical way to break it up would be to write three paragraphs. The first one would introduce the topic and the writer's opinion on it. Since the writer has two separate reasons for this opinion, why not put each argument in a paragraph of its own? The result would be three well-developed and easy-to-understand paragraphs.

Go back to the piece and see if you can tell where new paragraphs should begin. If you can see that a new paragraph should start with *First of all*, you are on the right track. The third paragraph should start with *Secondly*.

In the exercise that follows, you'll practice deciding whether the writer should use more than one paragraph. If only one point is being made, perhaps one paragraph covers the topic well enough. If, however, you find yourself wanting more detail and development, the writer probably needs more than one paragraph to get his point across. In addition, if a paragraph seems to be very long and to cover too many topics, you should divide it into separate paragraphs.

Exercise B: Is One Paragraph Enough?

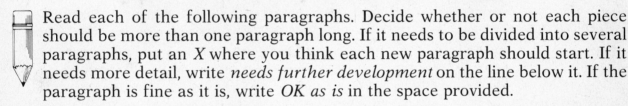 Read each of the following paragraphs. Decide whether or not each piece should be more than one paragraph long. If it needs to be divided into several paragraphs, put an *X* where you think each new paragraph should start. If it needs more detail, write *needs further development* on the line below it. If the paragraph is fine as it is, write *OK as is* in the space provided.

1. I'm getting really tired of hearing the same old things from the commercials on television. The sponsors must think I am not too bright when they repeatedly tell me that their products are better than others. One ad in particular that I cannot stand is the one that keeps repeating the phrase "ring around the collar." The chauvinistic man and his stupid-looking wife say the same thing at least a dozen times, and none of this makes me want to use the product. Another ridiculous commercial is the one in which a cat can talk and sing. Over and over again, this cat drums the name of the cat food into the viewer's head, in the hopes that he will run right out and pick up a case of it. My cat eats anything that is put in front of him, and no amount of repeating, "Meow," is going to get me to buy this overpriced stuff.

_____

Continued

2. My sister Jenny was being threatened by her ex-husband. My mother took in Jenny's son Tony. Jenny called the police and moved in with me. Now her ex-husband is awaiting trial.

_____

3. When Ed Morse turned fifty years old, he decided to live by the old saying "you're as young as you feel." He took dancing lessons with his fifteen-year-old daughter. He started taking his wife to new restaurants and to the movies. His son taught him to play frisbee. He decided that middle age might just be the prime of life.

_____

4. I have two decisions to make. The most important one is whether or not to quit my job. My boss wants me to have an affair with him, and he won't leave me alone. He even calls me at home. I want to quit, but I'm afraid it might take me a long time to find another job. The other decision I have to make is whether to move in with my boyfriend. I love him a lot, but I like being independent. I'm not ready to feel like I'm married. In addition, my parents would be horrified.

_____

5. The department is in good shape. Production is up 15 percent. Office procedures are being simplified. The workers seem to be happy. We may hire more people within the next month.

_____

ANSWERS CAN BE FOUND ON PAGE 12.

Answers

Exercise A

If your summary of the writer's purpose is not fairly similar to the one given here, look back at the paragraph. Is your purpose broad enough to include everything in the paragraph? Is it too general?

1. *persuasive*
   The writer's purpose is to: convince people to do volunteer work

2. *persuasive*
   The writer's purpose is to: tell people who work with young teens why they shouldn't ignore issues of drugs, sex, and alcohol

3. *narrative*
   The writer's purpose is to: tell a story about a spooky phone call

4. *informative*
   The writer's purpose is to: inform people about why a park is closed

5. *narrative*
   The writer's purpose is to: tell about walking home from work

6. *descriptive*
   The writer's purpose is to: describe someone's messy face

7. *informative*
   The writer's purpose is to: tell about improved treatment of cancer

Paragraph Highlight Exercise 1

Part 1

Here are some possible ways to finish the paragraphs. Use the guidelines in Paragraph Highlight #1 to check your work. Do your supporting sentences relate directly to the topic sentence? Does your concluding sentence, if you have one, tie the paragraph together and reemphasize the purpose?

1. We would like to have a clubhouse just for teenagers where we can have a snack bar and hold parties. We would like to be able to drop in there to meet friends to talk and study. This kind of place would really serve young people here.

2. If you move too fast, the other person may think you're more serious about the relationship than you really are. And if you commit yourself to someone before you're really ready, you may break someone's heart. All in all, it's best to take things one step at a time.

3. First of all, I don't like to study. Second, I was too fat to wear gym clothes. And third, I preferred working outdoors all day, even in the winter, to being cooped up in school.

Part 2

Here are possible topic sentences for the paragraphs. Make sure your topic sentences are broad enough to include all the rest of the sentences, but not so broad that the reader isn't sure of the purpose.

1. During times of financial crisis, my brother and sister had to work to help out my parents.

2. I'd like to show you our latest model of luxury automobile.

3. I know several married couples whose careers keep them from living together.

Exercise B

1. You should have put an *X* before the sentence beginning "One ad in particular . . " and another before the sentence beginning "Another ridiculous commercial. . . ."

2. *needs further development*

3. *OK as is*

4. You should have put an *X* before the sentence beginning "The other decision. . . ."

5. *needs further development*

2. Outlining

When One Paragraph Isn't Enough

A single paragraph is not always enough to cover your topic accurately or completely. Often you need to write more to get your message across. Longer pieces of writing can include everything from essays to personal and business letters to articles in organization (such as PTA or church group) bulletins.

A longer piece is similar in structure to a single paragraph. Both paragraphs and longer pieces have a beginning, a middle, and an end. Although there are no rules about how many paragraphs are necessary, a longer piece usually has these parts:

- introductory paragraph
- body paragraph(s)
- concluding paragraph

The introductory and concluding paragraphs act like a picture frame. They state the unifying idea for the entire piece. And they help the reader focus on the details in the body paragraphs.

Let's look at a piece of writing that has a lot of information packed into one paragraph but doesn't tell us much. This writer has been asked by his supervisors to write up a detailed description of his job duties so that they can determine whether his time is being well managed. Here is what he gave them:

> My present position at Ready Plastics is line foreman, and I have several important responsibilities. Most importantly, I am in charge of keeping the line operating as much as possible. I also am the link between the line repairmen and my line operators. In addition, I coordinate delivery and stocking of supplies for my line. These three basic responsibilities keep me very busy.

The writer gives us a great deal of information here, but we are left having to guess at a lot of things. The writer wanted to give a description of his duties and how he spends his time, but all he really did was write a paragraph listing the tasks. His description would be better if he described in more detail what each task involved.

Now we will look at the same job description that has been expanded to a longer piece. As you study each part of the longer piece, look back at the original description to see how its topic sentence and closing sentence were expanded.

Introductory Paragraph

An introductory paragraph has two purposes. First, it introduces the topic. Second, it lets the reader know what will follow in the body paragraphs. The introductory paragraph usually contains one sentence that sums up what the writer wants to say. This is called a **unifying statement**. It serves the function in a longer composition that the topic sentence serves in a paragraph.

In the process of introducing the topic and coming to the point, the writer also tries to get the reader's interest. He wants the reader to continue reading into the body paragraphs. The introductory paragraph is usually short, running about three or four sentences.

Here is an introductory paragraph for the job description you saw above. Notice how it has been expanded from the topic sentence in the paragraph.

MODEL
Introductory Paragraph

> My present position at Ready Plastics is line foreman, and my responsibilities fall into three general areas. I keep the line operating as much as possible, oversee repairs and maintenance, and make sure we always have enough supplies in stock.

The general topic introduced is the writer's job as a line foreman. The specific point, that he has three major responsibilities, is stated in the unifying statement.

Body Paragraph(s)

The middle of a longer piece, everything between the introduction and the conclusion, is called the **body**. It can be any length. The number of paragraphs in the body depends on how many ideas you want to discuss. You can write as many paragraphs as you need to make your unifying statement clear. Read the three paragraphs on job responsibilities below. Each is expanded from a supporting sentence in the single paragraph.

MODEL
Body

> Keeping the line operating at normal speed at least seven out of the eight hours on each shift is my most important responsibility. I have to make sure everyone on the line is trained and can keep up with the pace. I have to coordinate breaks so there are always enough people to keep the line moving.
>
> When something goes wrong with the machinery, the line operators call on me right away. I call in the repairmen and oversee the repairs to make sure the line gets moving again as fast as possible. I find out from them what caused the breakdown and what I can do to keep it from happening again.
>
> I inventory and order everything we need on the line. I count all the supplies once a week. Then I place orders. When the orders come in, I check the delivery to be sure I got what I needed. It's my job to be sure we never run out of anything.

Did you notice each paragraph in the body relates back to the unifying statement at the beginning? Each paragraph gives a description of one of the foreman's major tasks. Did you notice that the reason or main idea in each paragraph was clearly stated in a topic sentence? In the last paragraph, the main idea was also summarized in a closing sentence.

Concluding Paragraph

The end of a longer piece is called the **concluding paragraph**. Without a conclusion, a letter or composition remains a piece of unfinished business. Therefore, the concluding paragraph has two purposes. First, it restates the unifying idea from the introduction. Second, it summarizes the main ideas the writer used in the body to develop, explain, or prove the unifying statement.

In the process of restating and summarizing, the writer really comes full circle. That is, the writer ends with words and ideas that are similar to those used in the introduction. Then everything falls into place for the reader. The writer can also add some personal insights or follow up with a thought-provoking remark. Here is a concluding paragraph for the job description. Notice how the paragraph was expanded from the closing sentence in the original paragraph.

MODEL
Concluding
Paragraph

> These three areas of responsibility keep me very busy. A line foreman at Ready Plastics must check constantly to make sure nothing is forgotten. I'm a good foreman because I never stop moving.

You may have noticed that a longer piece of writing follows a very basic rule of good communication, written or spoken:

Tell your readers what you're going to tell them—*introduction*
Tell them—*body*
Tell them what you told them—*conclusion*

If you follow this rule, you'll get your ideas across. With the introduction you'll let your readers know what to expect. You'll give them the information in detail in the body. You'll remind them one last time in the conclusion.

Exercise A: Identifying Paragraphs

Look at each group of paragraphs below. They are not in order. Identify the introductory, body, and concluding paragraphs in each group. Write I for introductory, B for body, or C for concluding in the space provided after each paragraph.

1. Becky is driving down next week to start the process of settling us there. She will find an apartment for us and look for a job. We have some friends there whom she'll stay with for a week or so. They are sure she can find work quickly. I'll look for a job after we move, since I can't take time off before we go. _____

   I know you'll be sad to see us go even farther away, Mom, but I know you'll understand why we're doing this. Over the past year, we've become more and more sure that it's time to get out of New York. It's a great relief to us to make a decision. We'll keep you up to date on our plans. _____

   I'm writing to let you know of our plans to move to Tennessee in March. Jobs are scarce here in New York, and the cost of living is terribly high. We really think we have a better chance there.
   _____

2. What is most exciting to the American public, though, is the question of who will really get the office of president. Polls and surveys give us the answer to that question before the election is even over. But most of us still wonder if an underdog victory is possible. It has happened before! _____

Election years are always exciting. The coming presidential election is no exception. Candidates fly around the country attacking their opponents. They make promises about saving the Social Security system or bringing prayer back into the public schools. _____

Yes, election years are truly exciting years. Many people think that elections represent the grass-roots foundation of America. This foundation rests on the free choice of those who lead our country. Lots of people can get excited about that. _____

3. This is an apartment sublet agreement between Rachel Ward (the holder of the lease) and James Marchiano (the subletter). The sublet agreement will be in effect from June 1, 1985, to August 31, 1985. _____

James will pay 90 percent of each month's rent to the landlord by the first day of each month. Rachel will pay the remaining 10 percent. James will have the gas and electricity accounts placed in his name as of June 1 and will pay these utilities. James is liable for any damages done to the apartment during the period of this agreement. _____

The signatures of Rachel and James below show that both agree to these terms. Any additions or changes to this agreement must also be signed by both and attached. _____

4. We certainly do make billing errors from time to time despite our care to make sure each invoice is correct. And it keeps us on our toes to know that our customers are watching us as we go. Thank you for your input. _____

I'm glad that you wrote about your concern for the price that was charged for the calculator on invoice #4653. I checked into the matter for you. _____

According to our accountant, the amount billed is correct. The current price is $29.00. This was announced in a price adjustment letter on October 1. _____

ANSWERS ARE ON PAGE 31.

Exercise B: Writing Unifying Statements

 Read each group of related body paragraphs below. Each group lacks an introductory paragraph to introduce the topic and let the reader know what will follow in the body. Think of what might be in each introductory paragraph and write only the topic sentence for the introduction. As you learned earlier, this will be the unifying statement for the whole piece of writing.

1. One of my roommates is so neat that she won't let us put a bar of soap on the bathroom sink. She says it leaves a sticky spot. When I come home, anything I didn't put away before I left is lying on my bed. She hardly ever goes out, and when she does, it's usually with one of her parents.

   My other roommate is very good. She exercises at least four times every week. She eats three healthy meals a day and takes vitamins. She goes to bed early every night and gets up early in the morning. She reads the newspaper every day. Her long-distance phone bill is usually about two dollars.

   And then there's me. I usually get home after they've already gone to bed. I go grocery shopping about once a month. I travel every chance I get, so there's usually a half-unpacked suitcase on my bedroom floor. Even though I have a steady boyfriend, I always have a crush on some other guy.

2. If every house and apartment in America had one or more fire extinguishers, the number of fatal fires could be cut nearly in half. Most fires that break out in a kitchen or a furnace room could be put out right away by a nearby fire extinguisher.

   However, that isn't what happens. Firemen point out that the high price for an extinguisher is a poor excuse for not owning one. Quality extinquishers often are on sale for $10–$12. Sometimes fire departments offer real bargains for $6–$10. In some cities and towns, even those prices are subsidized if the home owner or renter is financially hard put.

   Some critics of fire extinguishers claim the average home owner or renter does not know how to use one properly. A person could spread the fire or get hurt while fighting the fire. However, firemen have proven that it takes about fifteen minutes of instruction to teach the average person to use a fire extinguisher properly and safely.

3. City regulations state that rental housing must be heated to 68 degrees at all times. The temperature in my apartment at 7:00 A.M. has been between 50 and 55 degrees every day for the last two weeks. It warms up about the time I go to work.

In the evening, the heat is on only until about 10:00 P.M. By midnight, it's 60 degrees and getting colder. I am not going to freeze silently any more. If the heat doesn't stay on all night beginning tonight, I will call in the city inspector.

SOME POSSIBLE UNIFYING STATEMENTS ARE ON PAGE 31.

Organizing Your Thoughts

Now you know about the parts of a longer piece of writing. But how on earth can you gather and organize all the ideas and details you need to write a longer piece? That's where outlining comes in. *Outlining* is just a way of organizing your ideas before you write. After you prepare an outline, you can write because your ideas are arranged in clear, logical order.

An outline is like a skeleton or a blueprint. It shows the underlying structure that holds the ideas of a composition together. Also, like a skeleton, an outline needs to be filled out with meat and substance. The writer adds details in order to make the writing come alive with meaning and interest. Preparing an outline can help you write a single paragraph, a long report, a letter, or even a short story.

Preparing an outline helps you get organized in four ways:

1. It provides a way to take inventory of what you know about your subject (*brainstorming*).
2. It helps you decide what additional information you need to find in order to fill gaps in what you know about your subject (*filling gaps*).
3. It helps you decide which information about your subject is not necessary to include (*irrelevancy*).
4. It provides a plan you can follow as you write (*outline*).

This chapter gives you some guidelines and steps to follow when preparing an outline. Remember that there is no best way to collect ideas or to put them into outline form. Some people have a set routine they prefer. Others find that their process changes somewhat depending on the type of writing. That's OK. The important thing is to let the process help you clarify and organize your ideas. Don't try to force your ideas to fit an outline. Your outline should be a tool that helps you, not a trap that restricts you.

Brainstorming

1. JOT DOWN IDEAS. There are lots of ways to get ideas flowing. You can talk to people, read an article or two, remember past experiences, ask yourself questions, keep a diary or journal, spend time observing, take notes, daydream, or just sleep on it. Regardless of what you do to get started, at some point you need to jot down on a "scratch sheet" all the ideas you can think of that are related to your topic. Jot them down in any old order or form, just as fast as they come to mind. Get as many ideas and details down on paper as you can. Just let your ideas flow—words and phrases. Don't worry about how the ideas fit or if they fit. That comes later. If one idea leads to another, put them both down. Somehow the more you write, the easier it is to think of other details to add.

However, if you get stuck before you finish, keep repeating the last word over and over until another idea comes. This takes concentration, but it usually works. Or take a break for a few minutes. Stretch, eat a snack, do something else for a while. When you return, reread your scratch sheet and new ideas should start to come.

Here's how a scratch sheet might look for the topic "reasons for selling our house."

neighborhood is too noisy   taxes getting too
                                              high here
don't need such   arthritis
a big yard   getting worse   could use extra
                                              cash we'd get
house too big to clean   from selling

never really   plumbing   market is good now
liked floor   never worked
plan   right
                          would like to be closer
                                to family

I like the garden we
have now   need a basement / garage
                     want more light / windows
                     would like a nicer view

2. GROUP RELATED IDEAS TOGETHER. Once you have jotted down plenty of ideas, put them together in related groups. This can be done by using symbols such as arrows, circles, and boxes. Or, on a separate sheet of paper, rewrite your ideas in organized groupings, putting related thoughts together. With practice, you will find a method that works best for you. Your goal is to group your ideas logically.

A few items may not seem to fit in any group at this point. That's OK. Just leave them for now. While you are doing your grouping, new ideas may come to mind. Great! Just add them.

Here is another look at the same sample scratch sheet after the ideas have been grouped together.

things wrong with the house

neighborhood is too noisy

don't need such a big yard

house too big to clean

never really liked floor plan

plumbing never worked right

arthritis getting worse

I like the garden we have now

taxes getting too high here — *economic reasons*

could use extra cash we'd get from selling

market is good now

would like to be closer to family — *things we'd like in a new house*

need a basement/garage

want more light/windows

would like a nicer view

3. IDENTIFY UNIFYING IDEAS. Now that you have your groups, the next step is to identify the unifying element in each group. What is it that the ideas or details in each group have in common? How do they relate to each other? By answering these questions, you can create a unifying label or heading to put near each grouping. Sometimes when you are creating headings, you'll see where to fit in some of the details that didn't seem to fit anywhere before. Fit them in now.

Once again, take a look at the scratch sheet. Notice that three headings—"economic reasons," "things wrong with the house," and "things we'd like in a new house"—have been added beside the groupings. In this case, the writer looked at each group of ideas and decided what the common element was. For example, the ideas "could use extra cash," "market is good now," and "taxes too high" obviously all relate to financial, or economic, concerns. The headings show how the random ideas on the original scratch sheet can be organized to provide an outline for writing several paragraphs.

Exercise C: Grouping Ideas

Part 1

Here are lists of brainstormed ideas. Group the related ideas in each list together by using circles and arrows or whatever works for you. See the model for grouping ideas on the previous page if you need help in getting started.

1. **TOPIC:** Reasons why I should quit my job
    not enough pay
    work hours too long
    boss is grouchy all the time
    can't afford to pay bills on the salary
    boss unfair
    boss plays favorites
    work too hard on back
    never get a raise
    no hope for advancement
    no insurance or other benefits
    don't have enough time with family

2. **TOPIC:** Vacations are necessary for most people
    get tired and bored with same surroundings
    burden of work can cause mental and physical
        problems
    can learn lots of new things
    good recreation
    doesn't have to be expensive to enjoy
    work efficiency improves
    help fight depression
    get to do things never done before
    rest mind and body

3. TOPIC: Fast-food is better than home-cooked meals
        no difficult preparation
        cheaper than grocery shopping
        not burned or undercooked like Mom's
        burgers and chicken better than meat loaf
        can have it whenever you want it
        can get burger and shake for $3.00
        can eat while you drive or walk
        french fries beat rice and beans any day
        don't have to pay extra for ketchup or salt

Part 2

Go back to Part 1. Choose a heading or name for each group. Remember to look at the ideas and try to see what they have in common. Then list your headings below. You may have more or less than the three headings provided for here.

1. TOPIC: Reasons why I should quit my job
        Heading A:
        Heading B:
        Heading C:

2. TOPIC: Vacations are necessary for most people
        Heading A:
        Heading B:
        Heading C:

3. TOPIC: Fast-food is better than home-cooked meals
        Heading A:
        Heading B:
        Heading C:

SOME POSSIBLE GROUPINGS AND HEADINGS ARE ON PAGE 31.

Exercise D: Brainstorming and Grouping Ideas

Six topics are given here. Choose <u>two</u> topics to brainstorm. For each topic, write down all your ideas. Then group the ideas that are similar. Finally, give each group a heading that tells what the ideas in that group have in common.

1. **TOPIC:** Advantages of buying your own house

2. **TOPIC:** Reasons for voting in a presidential election

3. **TOPIC:** Why rock concerts are good ways for performers and fans to "let off steam"

4. **TOPIC:** Reasons why nighttime soap operas have become so popular on TV

5. **TOPIC:** Disadvantages of raising the drinking age to twenty-one

6. **TOPIC:** Advantages of capital punishment in reducing crime

SEE PAGE 32 FOR A MODEL BRAINSTORM LIST AND GROUPINGS.

Writing an Outline

Once you have come up with a brainstorm list, you are ready to write your outline. Remember that what you write does not have to be final. You are free to make changes any time you choose. Your outline is not complete and final until you, the writer, decide it is. The steps below should help you plan your thoughts so that your reader will easily follow your writing.

1. PUT YOUR UNIFYING STATEMENT AT THE TOP OF A SHEET OF PAPER. Remember that the unifying statement will identify your topic and tell your reader what you want to say about it. You can write your unifying statement by refining the topic idea you brainstormed from. For example, if you are writing to a company to ask for a refund, the topic for your brainstorm list would be something like "refund for broken model airplane." Your unifying statement, therefore, might be something like:

> I am writing to request a refund for a model airplane I ordered, which was broken when it arrived.

You should end up with a clear and complete sentence that will unify your entire longer piece. After you have put it at the top of your outline, it will help you to double-check the relevancy of each idea you add to your outline. Paragraph Highlight #2 briefly reviews how to decide if an idea is relevant or irrelevant.

The unifying statement for the outline we've been working on might be "We should sell our house for several important reasons."

2. LIST HEADINGS BELOW THE UNIFYING STATEMENT. Once you have a unifying statement at the top of your outline, you will need to decide which groupings from your scratch sheet you should include. It's quite possible that you won't include all of your groups. It's quite all right to limit your topic in this way, as long as your unifying statement is an accurate statement of your main idea. Be sure that the groups you include provide enough information to make your final piece complete.

After deciding which groups to include, decide whether it makes a difference in what order you list them. Think about the different types of paragraph development you could use: time sequence, space, comparison/contrast, cause/effect, order of importance. The same types of development can be used in longer pieces too.

Then just copy your headings from your scratch sheet onto your outline under your unifying statement. List them in the order you want to discuss them in your writing. Leave several blank lines between each so that you can add your details there in the next step.

Here's how an outline based on the scratch sheet we've been using would look at this point. Notice how this writer chose to number her headings. You can use letters or numbers—anything that helps you see your organization clearly.

Unifying Statement: We should sell our house for several important reasons.

I. Things wrong with the house
II. Economic reasons
III. Things we'd like in the new house

When written as complete sentences, the headings listed under the unifying statement will become the topic sentences for the body paragraphs. Double-check. Are they all relevant to the unifying statement? Do they support, explain, or illustrate it? Are they listed in a logical order?

3. INCLUDE YOUR BRAINSTORMED IDEAS IN NOTE FORM. Take the ideas for each heading from your scratch sheet and copy them onto the appropriate places in your outline. Just use note form—simple words and phrases to list each detail. Later, when writing your piece from your outline, you'll expand these details into complete sentences to develop your body paragraphs. The details also should be listed in the most logical order to develop the paragraph they will be in.

At this point, you probably will have some details left over that will not be used in your outline. Some may not have fit into a grouping in the first place. Some may be repetitious. Leave out any details that do not fit.

4. SUMMARIZE MAJOR POINTS. The last part of the outline should be a few words in summary of your headings and details. This summary will become your concluding paragraph.

Here's the outline for "reasons for selling our house." Again notice that the writer has set off her headings with an organized system of numbers and letters.

Unifying Statement: We should sell our house for several important reasons.

I. Things wrong with the house
   A. yard and house too big to take care of
   B. plumbing doesn't work right
   C. never liked floor plan
   D. neighborhood is noisy
   E. tired of city

II. Economic reasons
   A. taxes too high here
   B. could use extra cash
   C. market is good right now

III. Things we'd like in new house
   A. basement or garage for hobby
   B. a nicer view
   C. more light and windows
   D. closer to rest of family

IV. If we sold our house now, we could buy one better suited to our current needs and interests.

Remember to be flexible. As new ideas come to mind, add them. Sometimes you will discover new angles of approach or come to new conclusions or think of better details. Change things as you write. Just double-check when you finish writing to make sure that everything still fits together logically.

PARAGRAPH HIGHLIGHT #2

In this Highlight, we will review how to get rid of irrelevant ideas in paragraphs and longer pieces of writing. Remember that relevant ideas support the topic sentence and irrelevant ones do not.

Look at the paragraph below and decide if it contains any irrelevant ideas.

Texas chili is fairly easy to make once you get the hang of how much spice you like. The whole process involves just browning some beef and onions and adding tomato sauce and spices. You can also add kidney beans if you'd like. Chili is great with corn bread. The spices include red pepper, black pepper, cumin, and chili powder. After trying it a few times, you should be able to tell exactly how much spice you can take.

Each sentence somehow relates to chili. However, this is not enough to make an idea relevant to the topic sentence and paragraph. Each sentence must support what is stated in the topic sentence or unifying statement. The sentence above, "Chili is great with corn bread," does not support the topic sentence. It may be relevant to eating chili, but it has nothing to do with how to make it. This sentence is irrelevant and should be taken out of the paragraph.

As you can see, you must beware of sentences that are related to a general topic but that do not support the topic sentence. This is where most errors of irrelevancy occur. Try the exercise that follows and practice detecting these imposters.

Paragraph Highlight Exercise 2

 Read each paragraph below and cross out any sentences that are irrelevant. If you are not sure if a sentence is relevant, decide what the main idea of the paragraph is. If the sentence does not support this main idea, it is irrelevant and should be crossed out. Not all paragraphs have irrelevant ideas.

1. You should look around before you choose a bank where you will open a checking account. Not all banks offer the same services, and one person's needs may be different from another's. For example, some banks offer free checking with an account balance of $500. This is ideal for someone with a large amount of cash. However, the person who does not have this extra cash should shop around for the lowest monthly fee that he can find. Savings accounts can vary from bank to bank too. Overall, checking accounts vary widely from bank to bank, just as needs vary from person to person. It pays to shop around.

2. Dick's new job didn't turn out the way he had thought it would. The advertisement boasted a large amount of responsibility and frequent chance for promotion. As it turned out, Dick was stuck in the filing office for longer than he thought. He also has not received a review in over a year. He had worked as a file clerk in his previous job at Centron. Dick's next move will be to speak to the personnel office or to look for another job.

3. Outside, it sounded like the gusts of wind would tear the roof off the house. Torrents of rain pounded against the house and streamed down the foggy windows. The whistling winds howled like angry wolves as the air grew colder and colder. No one was on the streets, and few cars had decided to brave the fierce weather. As the sky became darker, the rain began to turn to snow.

4. I think we need more space for the lunch room. As it is now, we have to eat in shifts, and half the time you still have to wait to get a seat. The present room should be expanded to at least twice its size. A new microwave would also be helpful. If the room is not enlarged, employees will be forced to eat out. This is unfair to everyone.

ANSWERS ARE ON PAGE 32.

Chapter Checklist

Does your outline have all of the following?

☐ a unifying statement
☐ headings related to the unifying statement
☐ all subheadings related to their headings
☐ enough information to make your point
☐ appropriate numbers and letters to make idea relationships clear

---

Exercise E: Completing Outlines

In this exercise you will be given two unifying sentences and "skeleton" outlines. Please fill in the blanks with your own ideas. Make sure each idea is relevant to the heading you put it under. If you have more ideas than the four spaces allow, simply add them on another sheet of paper. Remember, there is no correct number of ideas.

1. **Unifying Sentence:** Our large cities must find a way to cope with the alarming rise in crime.

   I. Types of crime that have increased during the past ten years
      A.
      B.
      C.
      D.

   II. Effect of increased crime on the people and property in the cities
      A.
      B.
      C.
      D.

   III. Some things the people and police can do to reduce crime in the cities
      A.
      B.
      C.
      D.

Continued

2. **Unifying Sentence:** An absolutely perfect day would be a day when three things would happen to me.

   I. All my debts would disappear
     A.
     B.
     C.
     D.

  II. Each member of my family would do one favor for me
     A.
     B.
     C.
     D.

 III. Could spend the day doing my favorite things
     A.
     B.
     C.
     D.

TWO COMPLETED OUTLINES ARE ON PAGE 33.

Exercise F: Writing Outlines

Below is a list of topics. Select <u>two</u> topics from the list or choose your own topics. Then write a unifying statement for each topic and prepare outlines of your ideas. You will use one of these outlines to write an essay in Chapter 3, so pick a topic that interests you. Refer to the Chapter Checklist to make sure your outline has all the necessary elements.

1. Why I plan to continue my education

2. The best time of the day

3. Caring for a baby

4. Writing a complaint letter to my landlord

5. Asking my child's teacher for an appointment

6. My opinion on legalizing marijuana

7. Qualities I admire most in people

8. Why employers should or should not provide free child care

AN OUTLINE BASED ON ONE OF THESE TOPICS IS ON PAGE 34.

Answers

Exercise A

1. B, C, I
2. B, I, C
3. I, B, C
4. C, I, B

Exercise B

1. It's amazing that I can live with two roommates who are very different from me.

   This unifying statement tells you why the writer is describing her roommates and herself: she's telling you why it surprises her that she can live with her roommates.

2. Everyone should own and know how to use a fire extinguisher.

   This unifying statement brings together the writer's opinion and the facts she presents. It clarifies the purpose of the piece for the reader, which is to convince you of something.

3. You must heat my apartment according to legal standards.

   This unifying statement specifically states what the writer wants to achieve by writing the piece.

Exercise C

Parts 1 and 2

Look over your answers. Check to be sure you have grouped together items that are related. Be sure each heading is broad enough to include all the items, but not too broad. For example, you could have grouped the ideas together with these headings:

1. Reasons why I should quit my job

   MONEY
   not enough pay
   can't afford to pay bills
   never get a raise
   no insurance or other benefits

   PROBLEMS WITH BOSS
   boss is grouchy all the time
   boss unfair
   boss plays favorites

   PERSONAL CONCERNS
   work hours too long
   work too hard on back
   no hope for advancement
   don't have enough time with family

2. Vacations are necessary for most people

NEED BREAK FROM DAILY ROUTINES
get tired and bored with same
    surroundings
rest mind and body
help fight depression
good recreation

NEED BREAK FROM WORK
burden of work can cause mental and
    physical problems
work efficiency improves

TIME TO TRY NEW THINGS
can learn lots of new things
get to do things never done before
doesn't have to be expensive to enjoy

3. Fast-food is better than home-cook meals

CONVENIENCE
no difficult preparation
can have it whenever you want it
can eat while you drive or walk

TASTES BETTER
not burned or undercooked like Mom's
burgers and chicken better than meat loaf
french fries beat rice and beans any day

MONEY
cheaper than grocery shopping
can get burger and shake for $3.00
don't have to pay extra for ketchup or
    salt

Exercise D

Model your work after the groupings and headings below.

TOPIC: Reasons why nighttime soap operas have become so popular on TV

MORE PEOPLE WORKING
can't watch daytime soaps
working people can relate more to situations on night soaps than on day
    soaps

BETTER ACTRESSES AND ACTORS THAN BEFORE
famous guest stars
more realistic acting than daytime soaps
can put more sex on at night

OTHER NIGHT PROGRAMS GETTING WORSE
too much violence on police shows
comedy shows getting boring

Paragraph Highlight Exercise 2

You should have crossed out:

1. *Savings accounts can vary from bank to bank too.*

    The topic sentence specifically refers to checking accounts, and therefore, a sentence about savings accounts is neither relevant nor supportive.

2. *He had worked as a file clerk in his previous job at Centron.*

    The topic sentence and all supporting sentences refer to Dick's dissatisfaction with his present job. Information about his former job does not support this topic.

3. *nothing*

    All sentences relate to the topic sentence.

4. *A new microwave would also be helpful.*

    The topic sentence specifically refers to the size of the lunch room. Improvements other than size, such as a new microwave, are not relevant.

Exercise E

Here are some ideas that could fill in the blanks. Check your answers to be sure they all relate to the headings.

1. Our large cities must find a way to cope with the alarming rise in crime.
    I. Types of crime that have increased during the past ten years
        A. illegal use of weapons
        B. sex-related crimes
        C. kidnapping
        D. drug traffic
    II. Effect of increased crime on the people and property in the cities
        A. decline in property value due to vandalism
        B. higher insurance rates for property
        C. people living in constant fear
    III. Some things the people and police can do to reduce crime in the cities
        A. lobby for gun control
        B. set up volunteer escort services
        C. insist that criminals be prosecuted, even in sensitive and personal situations
        D. give youth alternatives to gang membership

2. An absolutely perfect day for me would be a day when three things would happen.
    I. All my debts would disappear
        A. could charge on my MasterCard again
        B. Mr. Lyle at corner store would give me credit
        C. the electric company would stop bugging me
        D. would have cash to spend on clothes
    II. Each member of my family would do one favor for me
        A. Mom would make her famous broccoli casserole
        B. Dad would take me golfing
        C. Mary Elizabeth would lend me her jeans
        D. Maureen would keep her stereo low
    III. Could spend the day doing my favorite things
        A. bake pecan pies
        B. watch "Dynasty"
        C. shop for clothes
        D. sleep

Exercise F

Unifying Statement: I plan to continue my education because I will be able to do more for me and my family.

I. I will have a better future with my own career
   A. a high school diploma will mean a promotion and a raise
   B. improving my English and math will give me a chance for an office job in the future
   C. if my employers see that I want to learn, they will teach me more skills
   D. my children will see the benefits of education

II. I can take better care of my family
   A. I will be able to help support my parents when they have to retire
   B. my children can have better clothes and food
   C. we will have a house in a safe area with plenty of heat and hot water and a yard to play in
   D. I won't be so tired from having to do hard physical work

III. My children will have a better education
   A. I will be able to afford to help them go to college
   B. I will be able to help them with their schoolwork
   C. we will live where there are good public schools
   D. they will be able to start out in good jobs when they finish school

3. Writing a Rough Draft

What Is a Rough Draft?

You have learned that writing is a step-by-step process. Knowing your purpose and audience is one step, and drawing up your outline is another. Next, you will write a rough draft. The **rough draft** is the actual essay, letter, or memo you have been planning to write. It is your "first try" at putting your thoughts onto paper.

It is important to look at your rough draft as an unfinished piece of work. Why? Because chances are, when you see your outline expanded into paragraph form, you will want to make some changes. You may want to add a sentence or two or even take out a whole paragraph. You probably will also need to fix spelling errors, punctuation, and grammar problems. Don't worry. Fixing up your rough draft comes later in the writing process.

Don't use the word *rough* as an excuse to be sloppy in your work, however. You should always try to spell correctly and to use good sentence structure. Your writing will be easier to clean up later if you are careful now.

Why is the rough draft so important? This step in the writing process is where your ideas become complete sentences and paragraphs. At this point, you are really trying to communicate something to a reader. The previous steps you took were to help you, the writer, get your thoughts together. Now you are beginning to present them to an audience. For this reason, the rough draft is one of the most important steps of the writing process.

Using Your Outline

In Chapter 2 you saw how an outline can help you to organize your thoughts. However, the usefulness of the outline does not end there. An outline is not only a tool to organize your thoughts but also a plan to help you as you write. In this chapter you will learn to use your outline to write the first (or rough) draft of a piece of writing.

We will be expanding the following outline into a rough draft.

Topic: deciding to go back to school

Unifying Statement: The decision to go back to school was one of the most important and difficult ones I've ever had to make.

I. Didn't feel good about myself
   A. poor reading and writing skills
   B. no room for advancement in job
   C. friends had different interests

II. Fear of what might happen if I did go back
   A. failure
   B. be made fun of by younger students
   C. pressure on family

III. Had to make important choice
   A. friends encouraged and discouraged
   B. others my age had done it
   C. the final choice was mine

Conclusion: Although my decision to go back to school was one of the most difficult I've ever had to make, I believe it was a good one.

Turning an Outline into a Rough Draft

It will help you a great deal if you keep your outline nearby as you begin to write. Select one outline that you wrote in Chapter 2 and use it as you work through this chapter. When you have completed this chapter, you will have a rough draft based on your outline.

It will also help to leave big margins and write on every other line of the paper. This gives you room to add or change words and sentences right where they belong. You can see what you're doing, and you will have room to make lots of changes.

The following steps should help you write an organized rough draft.

1. USE YOUR UNIFYING STATEMENT TO DEVELOP AN INTRODUCTORY PARAGRAPH. Often, the unifying statement becomes the first sentence of the introduction. Then the rest of the paragraph tells what points will be made in the body to explain or support this statement.

We'll use this approach to expand our unifying statement into an introductory paragraph.

Unifying Statement: The decision to go back to school was one of the most important and difficult ones I've ever had to make.	The decision to go back to school was one of the most important and difficult ones I've ever had to make. Many other decisions I have made had an effect on my life at the time, but deciding to go back to school will affect my whole future. It was difficult to make this choice because I was afraid to take such a big step.

MODEL
Introductory Paragraph

Notice how the unifying statement becomes the first sentence of the paragraph. The following sentences support this idea and give a clue as to what will come in the body of the piece.

2. DEVELOP YOUR BODY PARAGRAPHS FROM THE HEADINGS ON YOUR OUTLINE. You can turn the outline headings into the topic sentences for your body paragraphs. Each idea under each heading becomes a supporting sentence in that paragraph.

Below is one way that our sample outline on the school decision could be expanded from the headings and subheadings. Notice how each idea from the outline is represented as a supporting sentence.

I. Didn't feel good about myself
  A. poor reading and writing skills
  B. no room for advancement in job
  C. friends had different interests
	I began thinking about school when I discovered I really didn't feel good about myself. My reading and writing skills were not good, and there was no opportunity for advancement in my job. My friends posed another problem. They weren't interested in the things I was, and this troubled me.
	
	Continued

MODEL
Body Paragraphs

Continued from page 37

II. Fear of what might happen if I did go back
A. failure
B. be made fun of by younger students
C. pressure on family

As I thought more about school, I found out that fear was my greatest enemy. I was sure I would fail. There I was, out of school for ten years with no hope of catching up. Besides, I would be with students who were young and smart. Then, there was the problem of pressure on my family. Could they put up with this kind of change? Probably not!

III. Had to make important choice
A. friends encouraged and discouraged
B. others my age had done it
C. the final choice was mine

The more I thought about it, the more I realized that I had a major decision to make. Then I asked my friends for advice. Some of them said I would never make it. Others pointed out that many people my age had done it and had succeeded. But the final decision was mine. At last I decided to go back.

Of course, you may want to add additional facts and ideas that are not listed on your outline. For example, the writer of the piece above mentions that he has been out of school for ten years. Although this fact was not included on his outline, it is useful information, and it helps develop the writer's ideas further. As you expand your outline into paragraphs, feel free to explain or support anything that you feel needs it.

REMEMBER: Use your outline to organize your writing. Don't let your outline restrict your thoughts and ideas.

PARAGRAPH HIGHLIGHT #3

No matter how well a paragraph stands alone, it is just one part of the whole. In order to do its part effectively, a paragraph must connect smoothly with the paragraphs around it. Think of a longer piece as a chain of islands. In order to get from one to the next, a bridge is needed. *Transition words* are the bridges that help your reader follow your main line of thought each time you make a shift in meaning and change paragraphs. Below is a list of helpful transitions.

Transition Words

however	in addition	nevertheless
on the other hand	moreover	consequently
first, second, last	for example	in fact
in spite of this	on the contrary	as a result

Let's look at some examples of how transitions can be added to the first sentence of a paragraph in order to link it logically to the preceding paragraph.

Imagine that the first sentence below is a topic sentence for a complete paragraph. Notice how the transition in the topic sentence of the following paragraph makes a logical connection to its preceding paragraph.

Children are a nuisance. —————————————— —————————————————————————— ——————————————————————————

Nevertheless, they are fun to be around. ——————— —————————————————————————— ——————————————————————

Without the transition *nevertheless*, it would not seem logical to move from a paragraph about children as a nuisance to one about children being fun to be around.

Take a look at the additional examples below. Notice how the transitions are incorporated into the sentences. And notice especially the logical connection that is made between the ideas of one paragraph and the paragraph that follows. The first sentence in each pair represents the topic sentence of one paragraph. The second sentence in the pair represents the first sentence of the following paragraph.

The new advertising campaign increased sales.——

In fact, this campaign was the most successful we've had.——

Tom Olson received praise for his efforts to improve safety on the line.———

On the other hand, he was frequently criticized.———

Our first step was digging the basement. ——

The **second** step was pouring the foundation.———

The last test was to check durability.———

In summary, our tests indicate that the new XL model is superior.——

Paragraph Highlight Exercise 3

The first sentence in each of the following pairs represents the topic sentence of a paragraph. The second sentence of the pair represents the topic sentence of the following paragraph. Choose a transition word from the list in Paragraph Highlight #3 that will make a smooth and logical transition between paragraphs.

1. The factory was bursting with frantic activity.
   _____, muscle-bound men and women lifted huge crates, while others hurriedly wrapped and stapled cartons.

2. Citizens of this district should vote for Guerrero for three good reasons.
   _____, Mr. Guerrero is the most qualified candidate.

3. Last Tuesday was one of the worst days of my life.
   _____, one good thing did happen.

4. Olga's son did really well in the track meet.
   _____, the young boy won every event he entered.

5. The primary concern of this committee is the care of our children.
   _____, we need to improve programs for the handicapped.

SOME LOGICAL TRANSITIONS ARE ON PAGE 44.

Exercise A: From Outline to Rough Draft

Part 1—Writing the Introduction

Using the outline you chose from Chapter 2, write an introductory paragraph for your essay. Remember to use your unifying statement and to set the stage for what will follow in the body paragraphs.

Part 2—Writing the Body

Again, use your outline and this time concentrate on expanding your ideas into body paragraphs. First, make each heading into a complete sentence that will be the topic sentence for each body paragraph. Next, expand your details to full sentences that support your topic sentence. Make sure each sentence supports the topic sentence clearly and effectively. To smooth out transitions between paragraphs, see Paragraph Highlight #3 for logical transition words you may be able to use.

TURN BACK TO PAGES 37-38 FOR INTRODUCTION AND BODY PARAGRAPH MODELS.

3. WRITE A CONCLUDING PARAGRAPH. Some people prefer to go directly from writing the introduction and body to writing the conclusion. Other people prefer to stop first and reread what they have so far. Rereading gives you a chance to decide if your writing says what you mean. You will also get a feeling for whether the body is generally complete. While the writing is still fresh, rereading sometimes reveals a gap that wouldn't be spotted later. Another reason to reread is to get a renewed sense of the whole piece. This usually makes it easier to write the conclusion, to decide what to say and how to say it.

Not all longer pieces need a separate concluding paragraph. For example, pieces two paragraphs long usually do not have a conclusion. In such cases, you can just add a summary sentence or two to the last body paragraph.

If a separate concluding paragraph is used, the topic sentence is usually a rewording of the unifying statement or the introductory paragraph. This isn't cheating, so go ahead and use this method. By the time a reader gets to your concluding paragraph, he probably would like a summary of your main point. Make sure you don't say it in exactly the same way, though. The following sentences of the concluding paragraph can summarize the piece's body paragraphs.

There are other things that can be added to a conclusion to make your piece end in an interesting, effective way. If it is a story, you can use a paragraph that tells "how it all worked out" or what happened after the main story ended. If you wrote a report, you may want to state personal conclusions you arrived at or suggest a next step to be taken or investigated. If your piece is persuasive, you may want to request help or suggest a change in behavior. There are many possibilities for tying everything together. Use your imagination and your own judgment as to what will best serve your overall purpose.

Using our outline and introduction again, here's an example of how this can be done. Notice the transition words used to signal that this is the conclusion. Also note the upbeat concluding sentence.

MODEL
Concluding Paragraph

Conclusion: Although my decision to go back to school was one of the most difficult I've ever had to make, I believe it was a good one.

Although making the decision to go back to school was the most difficult one in my life so far, I believe it was a good one. I carefully weighed the pros and cons. In spite of my fear, I knew I didn't feel good about myself as I was. I wanted to change. I wanted a chance at a better job. And, most of all, I wanted to stand for something in the eyes of my family, my friends, and myself! Returning to school made some of these things possible.

Exercise B: Writing a Conclusion

Reread what you wrote in Exercise A and write a concluding paragraph for that piece. Remember to restate the unifying statement from the introduction and then summarize the main points you made in the body paragraphs. Keep it short, and don't add any details that don't support your whole piece. You may also want to add an extra insight or thought to make your conclusion more interesting. If you'd like, try using one of the paragraph transitions from Paragraph Highlight #3.

COMPARE YOUR WORK TO THE CONCLUDING PARAGRAPH ABOVE.

Chapter Checklist

An organized rough draft should
☐ have an introduction that tells what the piece will be about
☐ develop the main ideas with one or more body paragraphs
☐ have a concluding paragraph or sentence that restates the main point of the piece
☐ use good transition words between paragraphs

Answers

Paragraph Highlight Exercise 3

Remember that transitions other than those given here can be used in some of these sentences. Just make sure your transitions make sense and represent the proper relationship between the ideas in the paragraphs.

1. The factory was bursting with frantic activity.

    For example, muscle-bound men and women lifted huge crates, while others hurriedly wrapped and stapled cartons.

2. Citizens of this district should vote for Guerrero for three good reasons.

    First, Mr. Guerrero is the most qualified candidate.

3. Last Tuesday was one of the worst days of my life.

    However, one good thing did happen.

4. Olga's son did really well in the track meet.

    In fact, the young boy won every event he entered.

5. The primary concern of this committee is the care of our children.

    In addition, we need to improve programs for the handicapped.

4. Narrating and Describing

Narrative Writing

Telling someone what happened is called **narrative** writing. Narrative writing can be anything from a letter to a friend about your first day at work to an entry in a personal diary or journal. In this kind of writing you may describe something or even give an opinion, but your main purpose is *to tell what happened.*

If telling what happened is your purpose, your outline will probably be a list of important events that you want to include. For example, if you want to tell what happened on your wedding day, you might organize your ideas like this:

Unifying Statement: My wedding day was one huge disaster from start to finish.

I. Morning of wedding
  A. 97 degrees in the shade
  B. hung over from night before
  C. mother in tears

II. The ceremony
  A. fiancée was a half hour late
  B. air conditioning in church broken
  C. two bridesmaids fainted

III. The reception
  A. caterer never arrived
  B. band turned out to be hard rock
  C. father and father-in-law got into fight

You should notice a couple of things about this organization. First of all, the events are listed in the order in which they happened. This makes it easier for the reader to follow. You will learn more about this type of organization later in the chapter.

Second, the writer does not include every single event that took place on his wedding day. For example, why didn't he include the fact that in the morning his father had given him $500 for his honeymoon or that a guest provided free champagne for everyone at the reception? Although these were, in fact, events that took place that day, the writer left them out because they do not support his unifying statement—his reason for telling the story. He is emphasizing the bad things that happened on his wedding day. To add in good things would take away from his purpose.

As you can see, it is important to choose which events you will include in your story. Don't try to include everything! Can you imagine how long and boring an essay would be if you included every little thing you did from brushing your teeth in the morning to taking your socks off at night? In the next exercise, practice choosing which ideas to include and which to leave out. Ask yourself if each idea really helps get your overall point across.

Exercise A: Choosing Events to Include

From each list below, choose the one event that should not be included in the essay based on the unifying statement given. Remember that, even though it happened, it does not necessarily support the unifying statement.

1. During my tour from San Francisco to New Orleans, I saw some absolutely beautiful sights.

    traveled down gorgeous Pacific coast

    spent a day at Grand Canyon

    went rafting on scenic Colorado River

    saw lush Louisiana bayou country

    visited a dreary ghost town

    traveled across vast golden farmlands

2. The following events led to the disturbance during our shift on Friday.

> Max Resnic was packing glasses
>> Sheila said she was feeling rather sick and wanted to go home
> mail truck arrived

Max said he would drive her home
> Max quickly stood up to help her
>> Sheila turned around and fainted in his arms
> Nanette Gireau walked in and saw them

Nanette slapped Max, who then dropped Sheila
> Sheila fell back and knocked 3,200 glasses on floor

3. The greatest day for me was the one when everyone did exactly what I wanted.

> boss didn't bug me
>> sons visited me without being asked
> neighbors kept their music low

husband let me sleep in
> it was sunny and warm outside
>> owner of Sal's Market let me pay with a check

4. My boyfriend, my daughter, and I loved our trip to the zoo Saturday.

> saw the lion tamer

petted farm animals for hours
> played on the wooden animal sculptures
>> laughed at the monkeys
> boyfriend worked that night

learned all about anteaters
> rode on donkeys

Continued

5. Working at the school carnival was not as much fun as I thought it would be.

> ran out of prizes
>
>   clown scared little kids
>
>   kids yelled and screamed
>
> we made a lot of money
>
>   was on my feet for six hours

ANSWERS ARE ON PAGE 59.

Sequence of Events

You probably notice that when you tell a story you tell everything in the order in which it happened. For instance, if you were talking about the fantastic play you saw in last night's football game, you would begin with what happened first, then second, etc. This order is called sequence of events, and it is very helpful to your reader. Look at the paragraph below and see if it is easy to understand.

PROBLEM:
Order

> The day I tried to buy tickets to the Springsteen concert was one hassle after another. By the time I got to the front of the line, I found out that there was a limit of four tickets per person! I decided to take the day off from work and buy about ten tickets for my friends and ten that I could sell at a profit. When I got to the stadium, I realized that I had forgotten my wallet. Of course, the day they went on sale I woke up two hours later than I wanted to. I stood in line for six hours in the pouring rain. What a day! That concert had better be good!

All the events of the day are given here, but they are difficult to follow because they are not given in the order in which they occurred. Take some time now and put this paragraph in the order in which the events took place. Doesn't that make it easier to understand?

Another helpful device that writers use to make their stories easy to follow is to use *transition words* between sentences and paragraphs. Transitions in narrative paragraphs are usually time order words and phrases that help indicate when something took place. Read the following paragraph, which does not include transitions:

> On his way home from the plant, Mr. Merringer witnessed an attempted car theft. He rode his bike through town, and he saw two women standing by a brand-new Camaro. He thought they must own the car. He noticed that one of them had a gun and was pointing it into the back of the other woman. The taller woman threw the other woman into the street in front of Mr. Merringer. He rode by. The thief jumped into the car and attempted to start it up. Mr. Merringer realized what was happening and quickly approached the car. The thief pointed the revolver at Mr. Merringer. A policeman arrived and arrested the woman.

PROBLEM:
No Transition Words

Although all of the events are in correct time order, the paragraph does not flow smoothly and easily. When does one action begin and another end? Now read the paragraph below with transitions indicated in dark type. Is this easier to understand?

> On his way home from the plant, Mr. Merringer witnessed an attempted car theft. **As** he rode his bike through town, he saw two women standing by a brand-new Camaro. **At first** he thought they must own the car. **Then** he noticed that one of them had a gun and was pointing it into the back of the other woman. **All of a sudden**, the taller woman threw the other woman into the street in front of Mr. Merringer **just as** he rode by. **Next**, the thief jumped into the car and attempted to start it up. **By that time**, Mr. Merringer realized what was happening and quickly approached the car. **While** the thief was pointing the revolver at Mr. Merringer, a policeman **finally** arrived and arrested the woman.

MODEL
Narrative with Transition Words

You now have seen the three most important aspects of narrative writing:

- include only events that support unifying statement
- use sequence of events order
- use transitions to help reader follow

Remember these three points when you do the exercise that follows.

Exercise B: Outlining a Narrative Piece

 You have just come back from a trip to another city where you stayed at a recommended motel. You were dissatisfied with your stay at the motel and jotted down the notes below to put into a letter to the motel management. After looking over your notes, you decided that they could be grouped into three categories: (1) your evening arrival at the motel, (2) the night spent there, and (3) the morning after.

Write an outline for the letter, keeping in mind that not all of your notes should appear in the letter and that you should use sequence of events order.

had to wait thirty minutes for desk clerk to get key

porter dropped my luggage and broke lock

very comfortable beds

temperature was very high

manager would not turn heat down even after being asked

Tim had never been to this motel before

couldn't get dinner room service although it was advertised

at check-out, overcharged $9.75 for calls I didn't make

took a shower after dinner in restaurant

never got my wake-up call

complimentary breakfast was cold

rent-a-car wouldn't start, and I couldn't reach rental company

too much noise in hall—couldn't sleep

AN OUTLINE BASED ON THESE NOTES IS ON PAGE 59.

Exercise C: Writing a Narrative Business Letter

Use the outline you wrote in Exercise B to write a business letter. You want to let the management know what happened to you from start to finish at this motel. However, remember to stick to the point of the unifying statement provided for you. Use the checklist on page 49 to make sure your narrative piece is a good one.

You will learn more about the proper business letter format in Chapter 5. For now, just put the address of the company you are writing to in the upper left part of your paper. Also include today's date. The name of the motel is Midtown Motel, and its address is 212 Marin Boulevard, Milwaukee, Wisconsin 77177.

Unifying Statement: I would like a refund for the night I spent at Midtown Motel because of the following events.

A GOOD NARRATIVE BUSINESS LETTER IS ON PAGE 60.

Exercise D: Writing a Narrative Piece

Choose only <u>one</u> of the unifying statements below and write a three- or four-paragraph narrative piece on it. For some of the items, you will have to choose one of the options from the parentheses. For others, you will have to complete the sentence first. Remember to draw up an outline before you begin writing.

1. My last birthday turned out to be (funny, sad, not what I expected).

2. The best time I ever had at a party was when. . . .

3. My first visit to the racetrack was a totally new experience for me.

4. I will never forget this year's (church, school) fair.

5. My favorite holiday last year was (Christmas, Fourth of July, New Year's Eve).

6. The day my first child was born was (hectic, a big surprise, the best day of my life).

7. The worst day I've ever had at work was the day. . . .

A GOOD NARRATIVE PIECE BASED ON ONE OF THESE TOPICS IS ON PAGE 61.

Descriptive Writing

Writing that describes a person, a place, an object, or an event is called **descriptive** writing. The purpose of this type of writing is to give the reader as accurate and vivid a picture as possible. The more detail you add to a description, the better the reader will be able to "see" what you want her to.

Remember that not all descriptive writing is visual. You can describe how something sounds, smells, and feels as well. The same principles apply to all of the senses: give the reader enough detail so that he can clearly get the picture, or feel, of what you are writing about.

Read the following piece and see if you get a very detailed picture from the description.

PROBLEM:

Not Enough Detail

> The inside of our favorite neighborhood bar is dark and quiet. You can see every table in the place when you step inside the door. Since it is never filled, you can always find whom you are looking for right away.
>
> The left side of the bar is where the regulars sit. Most of them are men, but occasionally a woman sits among them. This side is always more crowded than the other side.
>
> The right-hand side of the bar is where newcomers or passersby sit. Most of them are business people who are on their way home from work. They talk quietly among themselves and pay little attention to Evelyn and Mae, the twin waitresses.

You may be able to get a vague picture of this bar scene, but you may also have some questions about it. What kind of decor does the bar have? Is it new and sparkling clean? Or is it dingy and plain? And what about the regulars? Are they healthy construction workers or old street people? Do they look cheerful and talkative, or are they sullen and silent? How do you tell them apart from the newcomers?

These questions are only some of the ones that really descriptive writing should try to answer. If you really want your reader to see what you are writing about, you must include as much detail as you can. Now look at the improved description below.

> The inside of our favorite neighborhood bar is dark and quiet. The low ceilings and dim light try to disguise the dingy furniture and floor, but you can see the dust and feel the grit under your feet. You can see every fake wood table in the place when you step inside the old beat-up door. Since it is never filled, you can always find whom you are looking for right away.
>
> The left side of this run-down bar is where the regulars sit. Most of them are middle-age blue-collar workers from around the city, but occasionally a housewife or young diner waitress sits among them. They know each other well and laugh or chat while sipping out of cans and bottles. This side is always more crowded than the other side.
>
> The less-worn right-hand side of the bar is where newcomers or passersby sit. Long ago the jolly bartender made an attempt at dressing it up by putting plastic flowers on all the tables. The flowers are either missing or filthy by now and only add to the dinginess of the place. Most of the newcomers are well-dressed business people who are on their way home from work. They talk almost silently among themselves and pay little attention to old Evelyn and Mae, the twin waitresses.

MODEL
Descriptive Writing

Can you see that the bar has now taken on a little more life? We can picture it much more easily than we could from the first description. The writer has added a lot of detail and has chosen strong and descriptive words to get her picture across. Go back to the model and underline as many describing words and added details as you can. You'll learn more about choosing words in Chapter 7 of this book, but for now, concentrate on giving more details.

Exercise E: Giving Details

You saw how one writer took the original piece about the neighborhood bar and made it much more descriptive. Now you do the same. Use the same basic format to describe the bar, but add your own ideas and details to make the place come to life. Your bar might be big and noisy or glittery and expensive. Your regulars may be movie stars and famous personalities. Let your imagination run freely, but make sure your readers get the picture that you want them to get.

COMPARE YOUR WORK TO THE MODEL ABOVE.

Describing in Order

When you write a description of someone or something, you'll want to present your ideas in a way that helps your reader follow easily. In narrative writing, you saw that sequence of events was the easiest order for a writer to follow. In descriptive writing, you will choose from several different ways to organize your writing. Look at this outline for a description of a person. In what order are the ideas listed?

Unifying Statement: My grandfather is a picture of both old age and newfound youth.

I. Face and hair
  A. gray hair, but boyishly long
  B. tanned, wrinkled skin
  C. quick, bright smile

II. Upper body
  A. narrow, drooping shoulders
  B. lean build in sporty clothing
  C. no potbelly

III. Legs and movement
  A. slim and fit-looking
  B. slow but steady walk
  C. new gym shoes on feet

Were you able to tell that the order of details goes from top to bottom in this outline? This is one type of space order development. The writer intends to start out with the head and move to the feet. This is not the only order he could have chosen, but it will work well. The most important thing to do is make sure you _do_ have an order in mind before you begin describing. As a writer, you may have chosen to start at the bottom and move to the top for this piece. Great! As long as you present your ideas in some kind of order, your description will be understood. Paragraph Highlight #4 discusses some other ways to organize ideas.

PARAGRAPH HIGHLIGHT #4

So far in this book you have seen how to organize your ideas in sequence of events and space order. In this Highlight, you'll learn three more ways to arrange ideas: *cause-effect*, *order of importance*, and *compare-contrast*.

In *cause-effect* order, the writer states the causes of an action or feeling, then tells the effects brought about by these causes. Look at the example below and remember that the same order may be used in pieces more than one paragraph long.

The Red Sox victory over the Yankees in Fenway Park today had a big effect in the streets of Boston. The ten-to-zero no-hitter brought high hopes and huge celebrations to the Sox and their loyal fans. Taverns and local hangouts where folks watched the standing-room-only game were overflowing with happy patrons. The city mayor declared the following day "Red Sox Sunday," and sportscasters rushed to interview the star performers.

Can you see that the **Red Sox** victory is the <u>cause</u>, and that the rest of the paragraph tells you the <u>effects</u>?

When a writer uses *order of importance* in his work, he puts events, actions, feelings, or descriptions in order of how important he considers them. He may put the most important idea first, then give the less important ones. Or the writer may build up to his main point by putting the less important ideas first. Which order is used below?

My new girlfriend is everything I could ever hope for. She is a great cook, and she even enjoys making dinner every night. She shares my interest in hockey and auto racing, and she agreed to teach me how to play chess. Even better than that, she goes to services on Saturdays, which I really respect. But most of all, she's terrific because she demands the very best from me, and I need someone like that.

This writer chose to end with the most important idea.

With *compare-contrast* order, the writer tells similarities or differences or both between two people, things, or feelings. Here is an example of one kind of compare-contrast development in a paragraph.

> The way I feel in my therapy group is a lot different from the way I feel when talking to my friends or family. Even though you think you can be honest and open with close friends and relatives, it is nothing like a therapy session. In therapy, you are encouraged to discuss your very private feelings, and no one passes judgment or tries to influence you. If you tell a friend the same thing, he or she will usually try to change your mind or tell you you're wrong. Even though friends and family mean well, they cannot provide the secure and objective feeling that a therapy group can give.

In this paragraph, the writer uses *contrast* to tell how talking to her therapy group is different from talking to her family. If she had made a *comparison*, she would have showed how the two settings were similar.

Paragraph Highlight Exercise 4

 You can often write about the same topic with different orders of development. In this exercise, choose <u>one</u> of the topics below and write <u>two different</u> paragraphs, each using a different order of development discussed in this Highlight or elsewhere in the chapter.

1. The last movie I saw

2. My best friend's most annoying characteristic

3. How I look when I wake up in the morning

4. What I like least in a person

5. What I like most in a person

6. How I wish I looked

7. My favorite part of the day

TWO PARAGRAPHS USING DIFFERENT ORDERS OF DEVELOPMENT ARE ON PAGE 61.

Chapter Checklist

A good descriptive piece:

☐ gives plenty of detail
☐ puts ideas in logical order
☐ helps reader "see, hear, feel, smell, or taste" what you want him to

A good narrative piece:

☐ uses only events that support unifying statement
☐ uses sequence of events order
☐ uses transitions to help the reader follow

Exercise F: Outlining a Descriptive Piece

Choose one of the topics below and write an outline based on it. Remember to start by writing a unifying statement and to put your ideas in the order in which you intend to write about them. Also remember to use enough detail so that your reader will really get your point.

1. How you felt when a close relative or friend died

2. The least attractive man or woman you've ever seen

3. The sounds of your favorite or least favorite concert

4. The smells of an outdoor market

5. A busy, or a deserted, shopping mall

6. Your favorite outfit of clothing

7. An angry woman

8. The most beautiful thing you've ever seen

AN OUTLINE BASED ON ONE TOPIC IS ON PAGE 62.

Exercise G: Writing a Description

Use the outline you wrote in Exercise F to write a descriptive piece. Remember to refer to the Chapter Checklist to make sure your description is a good one.

A DESCRIPTIVE PIECE BASED ON THE OUTLINE CAN BE FOUND ON PAGE 62.

Answers

Exercise A

These are the events that do not support the unifying statement.

1. *visited a dreary ghost town*

   The unifying statement calls for details about beautiful sights, so a dreary ghost town wouldn't fit.

2. *mail truck arrived*

   The arrival of the mail truck would not have contributed to the disturbance that the writer is describing.

3. *it was sunny and warm outside*

   According to the unifying statement, the details need to be about people doing things the way the writer wanted them to.

4. *boyfriend worked that night*

   This detail is not related to the trip to the zoo.

5. *we made a lot of money*

   This detail doesn't fit in with the idea in the unifying statement—that working at the carnival was not fun.

Exercise B

Here is an outline based on the notes given. Pay close attention that you included only these ideas on your outline.

I. Arriving at motel
   A. had to wait thirty minutes for desk clerk to get key
   B. porter dropped my luggage and broke lock

II. Spending the night
   A. temperature was very high
   B. manager would not turn heat down even after being asked
   C. couldn't get dinner room service although it was advertised
   D. too much noise in hall—couldn't sleep

III. The morning after
   A. never got my wake-up call
   B. complimentary breakfast was cold
   C. overcharged $9.75 for calls I didn't make

Exercise C

This is a business letter expanded from the outline in Exercise B. Did you expand the ideas on the outline in a similar way?

December 4, 1984
Manager
Midtown Motel
212 Marin Blvd.
Milwaukee, WI 77177

To the Manager:

I would like a refund for the night I spent at Midtown Motel because of the following events.

On my arrival, I had to wait thirty minutes in the lobby while the clerk found the key to my room. Then, as we walked to the room, the porter dropped my luggage and broke the lock on it!

When I finally got to my room, it was very hot. I called the manager to get the heat turned down. He said it would be taken care of, but the temperature remained very high the whole time I was there. Meanwhile, I called for room service, which was advertised right in your lobby. I was told that it was not available and I would have to eat in the restaurant. After dinner, I was hoping for a peaceful night's sleep after a frustrating evening. However, there was a lot of noise in the hall, and I was disturbed all the night.

In the morning, I never received my wake-up call. After oversleeping an hour, I went to have my complimentary breakfast, which was cold. Then upon checking out, I found $9.75 on my bill for telephone calls I never made.

I think you'll agree with me that the service I received at your hotel was poor. I would like a full refund.

Sincerely,
Dorian McCarville

Exercise D

The following narrative piece is based on topic #5. Even if you chose this topic, your writing will obviously be very different. Notice how this writer put events in proper time order and used only ideas that support the unifying statement. Also note the frequent use of transition words.

> My favorite holiday last year was New Year's Eve. It was a wonderful day all day. I woke up in the morning excited because I had so many fun things planned. First I took a close friend of mine out to breakfast at a homey little diner. We ate omelettes and potatoes and Greek toast and drank coffee and talked and talked.
>
> Then at noon I went to pick up my fiance at work. We hit the stores, looking for things to dress up our New Year's Eve outfits. He bought a gorgeous blue and silver tie, and I bought some enormous black and gold earrings and white mesh nylons. It started getting late, so we headed to my apartment to get ready.
>
> We've never had as elegant an evening as that one before or since. Dressed to kill, we went to a wedding in a beautiful old church in a nearby small town. The reception was in an old restored Victorian house, and there was a buffet of unusual and delicious international foods. We ate, and we drank, and we danced to live music. Finally, long after midnight, we headed home in fresh new snow, the first of the new year.

Paragraph Highlight Exercise 4

You may want to review the types of development you chose to make sure your paragraphs are clear.

Cause and Effect

The last movie I saw, *Fiddler on the Roof*, left me feeling sad and quiet. Although at times the musical is joyous, in the last half the Russian Jewish family is torn apart by events of history. The haunting songs brought tears to my eyes, and the tragic faces of the characters are still etched in my mind. The movie really allowed me to experience what life might have been like in another time and place.

Order of Importance

Fiddler on the Roof, the movie I saw most recently, is an outstanding film. The scenery ranges from beautiful to very harsh, depending on the effect that's needed in a scene. The music and songs sweep you up into what's happening on the screen. The story is sad and haunting. But the characters themselves are the most powerful aspect of the movie. You rejoice and mourn with them as they struggle to deal with a changing world.

Exercise F

This outline is based on topic #6.

Unifying Statement: In my favorite outfit, the most comfortable clothes I own, I'm ready for anything.

I. My favorite kind of clothes
   A. feel ready for anything in favorite clothes
   B. like to dress in loose, soft, old clothes

II. Each part of the outfit
   A. shirt
   B. sweater
   C. jeans
   D. tennis shoes

III. It lets me get things done
   A. nothing's in the way
   B. can move around any way I need to
   C. don't have to worry about the clothes

IV. How I feel when I'm wearing it
   A. fast and strong
   B. able to do anything
   C. ready to get to work

Exercise G

Compare this piece of writing to the outline from Exercise F. Then compare your writing to your outline. Did you develop your ideas clearly and effectively?

In my favorite outfit, the most comfortable clothes I own, I'm ready for anything. I like clothes that fit loosely. I also like clothes that are soft and old and have been washed many times.

Each part of my favorite outfit has a lot of character. My red cotton turtleneck is soft enough to wash a baby with. I've had my big gray wool sweater since I was eleven. My jeans are faded and faithful Lee Riders. My comfy tennis shoes make me feel like I'm walking on air.

When I'm in my favorite outfit, nothing I'm wearing gets in my way, and I can move freely. I don't have to worry about the clothes because they're already old and I know how tough they are.

In fact, when I'm wearing my favorite outfit, I feel fast and strong. I'm ready for anything. Just tell me what to do, and I'll roll up my sleeves and get to work.

5. Informing and Persuading

Informative Writing

You use **informative** writing when you explain something to someone, whether it be giving directions to the gas station or explaining the effects of a new wage scale at work. Informative writing does one of four things:

1. gives directions
2. explains "how to"
3. answers questions who, what, where, when, and how
4. makes something easier to understand

If you decide that your purpose is to inform, keep in mind several things as you write.

1. PRESENT THE FACTS, NOT YOUR OPINIONS. Whether you are writing a business memo or instructions to the telephone repairman, your writing will be clearer if you stick to answering who, what, when, how, and where. Leave your point of view out unless you are asked for it.

2. PRESENT YOUR FACTS CLEARLY AND MAKE THEM TO THE POINT. Remember that you are giving information in answer to who, what, when, how, and where. Be precise with your names, dates, and figures so that your reader does not have to make any guesses. Your purpose is to make your reader understand something. If you clutter your facts with unrelated ideas, the reader will become frustrated and confused.

3. PUT YOUR WRITING IN THE APPROPRIATE FORMAT. Depending upon the situation and the reader, there may be a preferred format for your writing. For instance, if you are writing a job memo, make sure you include the name of the person you are writing to. Also, include your own name right up front. A reader should be able to see right away whom the memo is for and who has written it. In the models section of this book you will see many different writing formats that can be used in both personal and business writing.

Writing a Job Memo

Look at the job memo below and decide if it accomplishes its informative purpose effectively. The writer was asked by the plant manager to summarize some changes that were made in her department.

PROBLEM:

Poor Job Memo

Mr. Pruitt:

My name is Isabel Valderez, and I am writing to inform you of some changes we have made in the printing department since our last meeting. I feel that they are good changes and that you will approve of them wholeheartedly. Everybody in the department is looking forward to trying out the new system.

First of all, every request for prints will have to be approved by the pretty young woman who sits closest to the back door. She doesn't mind this extra duty, and frankly, I think she's the best for the job. What a hard worker she is!

Second, the last person on the shift each day will be in charge of logging in all filled requests. Sometimes that person is Lottie Bates, sometimes it is Ted Beauregard, and occasionally others fill in. Personally, I think we could even ask the night shift people to help out with this, but the others decided just to go with the day shift. With this system, we can cut back on our costs, which I think really ought to be the focus of this quarter.

If you have any questions, please call me anytime. I think you are doing a great job as manager, and I often talk about the great things you do for us.

Do you think the plant manager found this memo informative and to the point? Probably not. Some of the information that he wanted is in the memo, but it is buried under lots of opinions and irrelevant material. In addition, the writer does not mention any specific dates and names when they are important. If Mr. Pruitt is as busy as most plant managers, he probably had little time to figure out the important points in this memo.

Let's look at the same memo, much improved. Notice how the three points made above are carried through. The writer (1) presents facts, not opinions; (2) states facts clearly and to the point; and (3) uses an appropriate format. The important features of an informative job memo are pointed out to you.

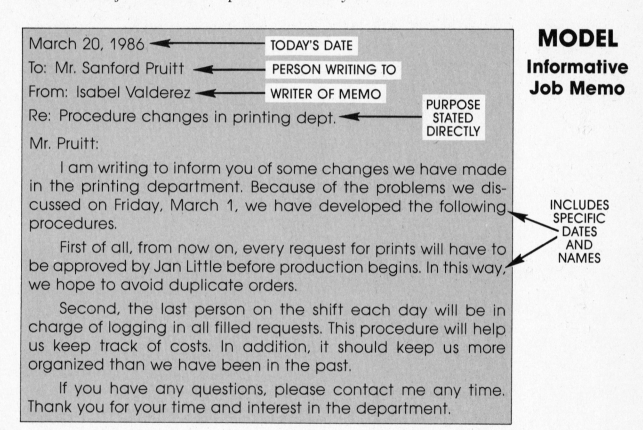

MODEL
Informative Job Memo

March 20, 1986 ← TODAY'S DATE
To: Mr. Sanford Pruitt ← PERSON WRITING TO
From: Isabel Valderez ← WRITER OF MEMO
Re: Procedure changes in printing dept. ← PURPOSE STATED DIRECTLY
Mr. Pruitt:

I am writing to inform you of some changes we have made in the printing department. Because of the problems we discussed on Friday, March 1, we have developed the following procedures.

First of all, from now on, every request for prints will have to be approved by Jan Little before production begins. In this way, we hope to avoid duplicate orders.

INCLUDES SPECIFIC DATES AND NAMES

Second, the last person on the shift each day will be in charge of logging in all filled requests. This procedure will help us keep track of costs. In addition, it should keep us more organized than we have been in the past.

If you have any questions, please contact me any time. Thank you for your time and interest in the department.

Exercise A: Writing a Job Memo

Imagine yourself in the position of chief clerk at a clothing outlet. Your supervisor, Donna Mahan, has asked you to write up a memo summarizing what you feel are the major problems for the twenty-five clerks you work with. You have drawn up the following notes. Now write a job memo, using these notes and the model memo on page 65 to help you. Since the notes are not in any order, you will probably want to reorganize them and write an outline before you begin writing. Remember that only the relevant notes should be included in your final piece.

> shifts are too long, and clerks can get irritable with customers

not enough incentive to stay with the company

> Marco Swanzey thinks pay is low, but he's a jerk anyway

> deliveries made too late in day, so on-duty clerks can't finish unpacking by closing time

September 1st, 9th, and 10th the registers were left with too little cash to service our needs, and it happens several times a month

> I think we have a pretty good staff all around

we are frequently understaffed at sale time

A MODEL JOB MEMO IS ON PAGE 83.

Writing a Business Letter

Many letters you write to companies or formal organizations are informative. Such letters require a very specific format. This format is important because it makes a good impression on the reader. The three principles described on pages 63 and 64 hold true for an informative business letter:

1. Present facts, not opinions. (Later, in persuasive writing, you will learn the best way to express your personal point of view.)
2. Present your facts clearly and specificly.
3. Use the appropriate format.

The following model shows you the important elements of a business letter. You will see other business letters for many different purposes throughout this book.

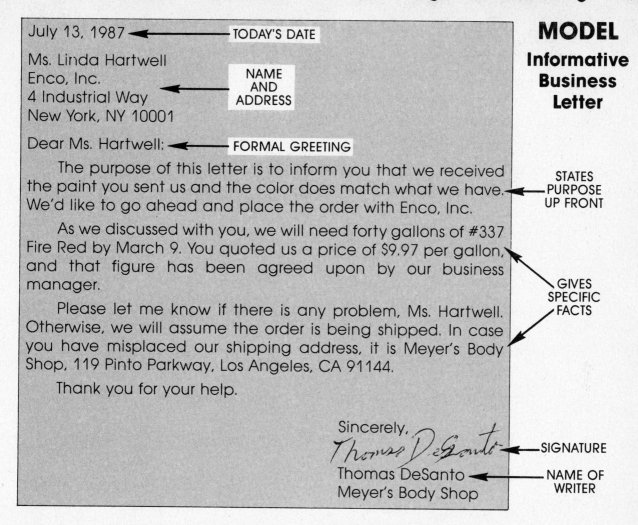

MODEL
Informative Business Letter

July 13, 1987 ◄———— TODAY'S DATE

Ms. Linda Hartwell
Enco, Inc. ◄———— NAME AND ADDRESS
4 Industrial Way
New York, NY 10001

Dear Ms. Hartwell: ◄———— FORMAL GREETING

 The purpose of this letter is to inform you that we received the paint you sent us and the color does match what we have. ◄——— STATES PURPOSE UP FRONT We'd like to go ahead and place the order with Enco, Inc.

 As we discussed with you, we will need forty gallons of #337 Fire Red by March 9. You quoted us a price of $9.97 per gallon, and that figure has been agreed upon by our business manager. ◄——— GIVES SPECIFIC FACTS

 Please let me know if there is any problem, Ms. Hartwell. Otherwise, we will assume the order is being shipped. In case you have misplaced our shipping address, it is Meyer's Body Shop, 119 Pinto Parkway, Los Angeles, CA 91144.

 Thank you for your help.

        Sincerely,

        Thomas DeSanto ◄——— SIGNATURE
        Thomas DeSanto ◄——— NAME OF WRITER
        Meyer's Body Shop

Notice how the writer stuck to his point and gave specific information. The reader will have no trouble quickly understanding this letter.

The body of a business letter will change depending on your purpose. However, the standard features of a business letter, pointed out for you above, will remain the same. Now do the next exercise for some practice in writing informative business letters.

Exercise B: Writing an Informative Business Letter

Write a business letter in reference to the situation described below. Keep in mind what you know about informative writing as well as writing business letters.

You have been offered a job as an inventory clerk at Prontess Company and have decided, after some thought, that you will take the job. The personnel officer at Prontess has asked you for a written confirmation that you will start on February 15 at the starting salary of $350 per week. You also must let him know whether you will participate in the group health insurance plan provided by Prontess Company.

The name of the personnel officer is Reginald Tierson. The address at Prontess is 444 Lester Boulevard, Memphis, Tennessee 21010.

AN INFORMATIVE BUSINESS LETTER IS ON PAGE 83.

Writing Directions and Other Informative Pieces

You probably have had to give someone directions or instructions many times in your life. When you write directions to your house or instructions on how to start dinner, you are writing an informative piece.

Most often, this kind of writing does not require the formal setup that job memos and business letters do. However, the same principles of good informative writing still hold true. Obviously, if you are leaving a note to the baby-sitter, you do not need to use a formal name and address format in the piece, but you must still write to be understood.

Here is a copy of a note to a teacher informing him why one of his students was absent. Do you think it is good informative writing?

PROBLEM:
Poor Informative Note

> My child was not in school because he had a toothache and had to be taken to the dentist. He had been feeling a lot of pain over the past few weeks, and I finally realized why. When his brother Bob had the same problem, it took me three months to figure out what it was! I'm actually a good father, although sometimes you wouldn't know it!

Unfortunately, some important information is missing from this note. First of all, which teacher is it supposed to go to? Even if the note is handed to the right person, the name of the person being written should always appear somewhere! Second, it is always safe to include the name of the child and the dates he was absent. If the note is misplaced and picked up by a stranger, the reader will have no idea to whom it referred. In addition, always sign your name to your writing.

The other problem is not missing information, but irrelevant information. The sentences about Bob's illness and whether or not the writer is a good father are not useful information for the teacher. They are better left out. Here is an improved note to a teacher.

MODEL
Note to Teacher

> October 6, 1986
>
> Dear Mr. Jenkins,
>
>   Please excuse the absence of my daughter, Danita Blain, on October 4 and 5. She had a bad cold.
>
>   Sincerely,
>
>   Tony Blain

An effective informative piece

- sticks to facts, not opinions
- answers questions who, what, when, how, and where
- presents specific facts clearly and to the point
- uses the proper format

Exercise C: Giving Directions

Choose <u>one</u> of the following situations and write directions. Keep in mind what you know about informative writing and the format it should take.

1. You have called Bruce, the building maintenance manager, about some repairs that need to be made in your apartment. You will be out when he arrives, so he has asked you to jot down what the problems are. You need to tell him (1) what is wrong with the drain in the bathroom sink (the large bathroom, not the small one); (2) what happens when you try to open the window on the right wall of the kitchen; and (3) that the thermometer never reads more than sixty degrees, but the apartment is always very hot.

2. Your friend has asked you to write down the directions to the food warehouse where you shop. She will need to take a bus part of the way, then walk. Make up some directions and be very specific. Your friend has lots of trouble following directions.

3. You are leaving your car at the repair garage with a note about what you need fixed. Make up three things that could be wrong with an automobile and write a note telling the repairman that these are the three problems you are having. Be specific and make sure you state what you would like done.

AN INFORMATIVE PIECE BASED ON ONE OF THESE SITUATIONS IS ON PAGE 84.

Persuasive Writing

Persuasive writing is any writing in which you give your opinion and support it. You are persuading your reader to see your point of view and possibly take some action on it.

You use persuasive writing in many different situations. For example, a business letter in which you complain about a product and ask for a refund is persuasive writing. A letter to the editor of a newspaper about a political issue is persuasive writing. Many times you are asked to give your point of view and support it on writing tests. This is also an example of persuasive writing.

These are the three main points to remember when you write a persuasive piece:

1. STATE YOUR OPINION CLEARLY IN YOUR INTRODUCTORY PARA-GRAPH. Don't beat around the bush and hide your point of view with unclear ideas. There is never any right or wrong in persuasive writing, so don't be afraid to be clear and forceful right up front.

Keeping this in mind, which of the following is a better introductory paragraph? The writer has been asked to state whether he agrees or disagrees with the idea of capital punishment and to support his position.

Concerning the issue of capital punishment, I believe it is a very complex situation. On the one hand, we want justice for the victim. On the other hand, murder is murder. Whether a man should be put to death for killing his neighbor is a question that has plagued man for years.

PROBLEM:
No Opinion Stated

Capital punishment is the only solution we have to stop the senseless crimes in our country. I believe it is the only way we can convince the criminal that law is law, and we mean business. History has told us that long prison terms do not prevent men and women from killing one another.

MODEL
Opinion Stated Clearly

Can you see that the second paragraph is a better introduction to a persuasive piece than the first one? Look closely at the first, and you will see that no point of view is given. The reader has no idea of the writer's opinion, and therefore it is not persuasive writing.

Whether or not you agree with the concept of capital punishment, the second paragraph is the better introduction. We know the writer's position, and we are ready to hear him defend it. Writers are often afraid to come out and say what they think.

They think that by not committing themselves they will make everyone happy. This is not the case. In persuasive writing, you must take one point of view and stick to it. Your purpose is to convince the reader that your position is the best one.

2. *SUPPORT YOUR VIEWPOINT WITH GOOD REASONS.* These reasons can be facts or personal experiences that back up your position in any way. For instance, if you were trying to convince a company that it should refund your money for a defective flashlight you purchased, what reasons would you give? You must be specific and convincing.

3. *SUMMARIZE YOUR POINT OF VIEW IN A CLOSING PARAGRAPH.* Sometimes this conclusion need only be a sentence or two. The purpose of it is just to reinforce your position in the mind of the reader.

Look at the business letter below and decide if this company would be persuaded by this writing.

PROBLEM:

Poor Complaint Letter

> Dear whoever is in charge,
>
> Last night was one of the coldest of the year. Our electricity went out, and I had to go out to the garage to fix some fuses. You can imagine how enraged I was when my brand-new flashlight didn't work.
>
> Give me my money back, or I will take this matter to the police.
>
> Jake Renfrue

As you already know, this is not a good format for a business letter. The writer should have included the name and address of the company, as well as his own name and address and the date. In short, a letter of complaint should have a more formal format.

Besides the format, however, this letter has other problems. The writer has left out important information and included some irrelevant information. For example, the long description of the night the flashlight failed to work is surely not of interest to the company. The writer takes away from his purpose by including this extra information. Second, some additional facts about what kind of flashlight it is, where and when it was purchased, and exactly what was wrong with it would certainly help to persuade the reader more.

The last thing wrong with this letter is its accusing tone. There is no need for the writer to threaten to call the police before he even sees what the company will do for him. Although you want to be firm and direct in a letter of complaint, you should not use an unnecessarily angry tone. Look at the improved letter below.

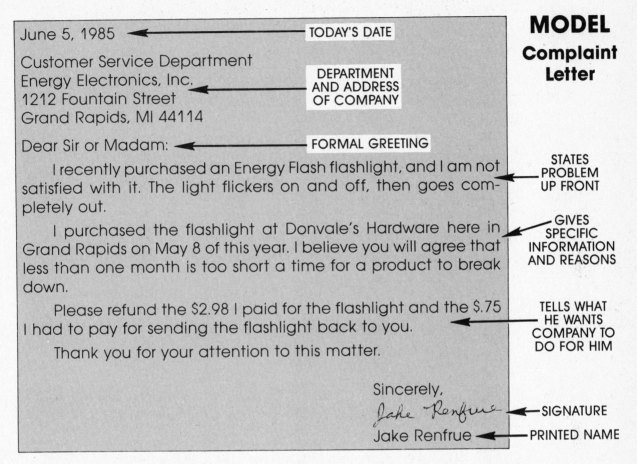

MODEL Complaint Letter

June 5, 1985 — TODAY'S DATE

Customer Service Department
Energy Electronics, Inc. — DEPARTMENT AND ADDRESS OF COMPANY
1212 Fountain Street
Grand Rapids, MI 44114

Dear Sir or Madam: — FORMAL GREETING

I recently purchased an Energy Flash flashlight, and I am not satisfied with it. The light flickers on and off, then goes completely out. — STATES PROBLEM UP FRONT

I purchased the flashlight at Donvale's Hardware here in Grand Rapids on May 8 of this year. I believe you will agree that less than one month is too short a time for a product to break down. — GIVES SPECIFIC INFORMATION AND REASONS

Please refund the $2.98 I paid for the flashlight and the $.75 I had to pay for sending the flashlight back to you. — TELLS WHAT HE WANTS COMPANY TO DO FOR HIM

Thank you for your attention to this matter.

Sincerely,

Jake Renfrue — SIGNATURE

Jake Renfrue — PRINTED NAME

The format of this letter is much better. In addition, the writer gives specific names and dates and uses a pleasant, but firm, tone. This letter is more likely to persuade the reader than the previous one.

The next exercise will allow you to practice writing complaint letters like the one above. Remember to state your point of view (your complaint) up front, then support it with concrete reasons.

Exercise D: Writing a Letter of Complaint

Write a complaint letter in reference to the situation described below. Be sure you keep in mind the correct format as well as what makes good persuasive writing.

You bought two frozen pizzas at your usual grocery store. When you opened them up, you found one of them covered with mold. Because your grocery store is very reliable, you decide not to take it back, but to write to the pizza company instead.

The brand name of the pizza is Naomi's Parlor, and the batch number you find listed on the box is 03178. You paid $2.76 for the pizza on June 9.

The address for Naomi's Parlor is 665 West Burlington Street in Midtown, Ohio 52134.

A MODEL LETTER OF COMPLAINT IS ON PAGE 84.

Essay Assignments or Tests

Often on writing tests or assignments you will be given a situation and asked to give your opinion on it. You will have to be as persuasive as possible in a limited amount of space or time or both. If you remember the three basic rules of thumb for persuasive writing, you will have a good head start. Here are some other hints to help you be as convincing as you can be.

1. ALTHOUGH YOU MAY NOT HAVE TIME TO WRITE DOWN AND REVISE A COMPLETE OUTLINE, DO TRY TO USE A BRAINSTORM LIST. If you start writing right off the top of your head, your writing will show that you did not organize your thoughts. Once you have determined the situation and your opinion on it, jot down the reasons for your point of view. Then try to group together those that are similar—those that you will use in the same paragraph.

2. PRACTICE TAKING A STAND ON ISSUES THAT YOU MAY NOT FEEL PARTICULARLY STRONG ABOUT. Remember that, on an essay test or assignment, part of your job is to state your opinion clearly. As you saw earlier in this section, an introduction that gives both sides of an issue without choosing one or the other is not persuasive. If an essay situation asks you to say whether the sky should be pink instead of blue, you may not really care. Force yourself to take a position so that you can defend it.

3. MAKE SURE YOUR REASONS ARE GOOD ONES. As we discussed before, reasons can be anything from researched facts to personal knowledge or incidents. For example, if you were trying to convince someone that first aid courses can help save lives, you could use two types of reasoning. First of all, you could give statistics about how many lives have been saved by people who know first aid. Another way to support your topic sentence could be to tell about how your grandmother was saved from choking to death by a cousin who had taken a first aid course. You can use a combination of both personal incidents and researched facts. Use whatever is convincing.

Be sure that your supporting sentences are real reasons, not just a restatement of your opinion. Writers sometimes are so sure of their position that they simply repeat it over and over. They forget that the reader needs evidence to see their point of view. For example, read the following paragraph. Decide if the supporting sentences give good reasons for the opinion in the topic sentence.

> The nuclear arms race is the biggest single problem our country faces today. There is no bigger problem. All other problems we have in society today are small compared to the ever-present threat of nuclear war. Crime, hunger, and ignorance are insignificant compared to the arms race. Nuclear arms represent society's biggest problem because they have caused a lot of trouble since they were first used.

PROBLEM:
No Supportive Reasons

We are sure of the writer's opinion, but she is not very convincing. She states over and over that the nuclear arms race is society's biggest problem, but she doesn't say why this is so. She gives no statistics or other facts to back up her point of view.

The writer's statement that nuclear arms are the biggest problem because they have caused a lot of trouble doesn't really say anything. The writer is simply restating her opinion to support her opinion. This problem can occur in your writing if you do not organize well. Remember that each supporting sentence must give enough evidence to convince the reader. Can you see why this paragraph is much improved over the last one?

> The nuclear arms race is the single biggest problem facing our country today. While we may see crime and pollution as big problems, neither of these is capable of wiping out the whole human race. Our society is working toward reducing crime, ignorance, and poverty, but it does little to put a stop to the arms race. Statistics show that, while an average of twenty people are murdered each day, over two million can be destroyed by one nuclear warhead in a matter of seconds. There is no question about what is the greatest threat to mankind.

MODEL
Gives Specific Reasons

In this paragraph, the writer tells us why he believes the arms race is a bigger problem than crime or poverty. We may not agree with him, but he <u>does</u> give reasons for his position. Furthermore, he provides a statistic for his statement that nuclear war is a greater danger than crime. In short, each sentence gives the reader more information to support an opinion. This is good persuasive writing.

In the next exercise, practice using supportive evidence instead of just restating an opinion. A good test to see whether a reason is just a restatement of an opinion is to put an equal sign between the two ideas and see if they are, in fact, the same. If they are the same, then the second idea is <u>not</u> a reason for the first. For example, does this sentence give <u>evidence</u> for the opinion?

> My favorite color is blue because I like it more than any other color.

Use the equals sign to help you decide:

> My favorite color is blue $\overset{?}{=}$ I like it more than any other color.

Can you see that the two ideas mean the same thing? This sentence does not give any support to the statement that the writer's favorite color is blue. Now look at the following sentence.

> My favorite color is blue because it matches my eyes.

Try the equal sign trick:

> My favorite color is blue $\overset{?}{=}$ it matches my eyes.

As you can see, these two ideas are not the same. In fact, the second part of the sentence gives a sound reason for the first part. It tells the reader <u>why</u> blue is the writer's favorite color.

Exercise E: Supporting an Opinion

Each of the following sentences states an opinion and gives a reason for that opinion. Decide whether the reason given is good supportive evidence or just a restatement of an opinion. To do this, use the equal sign method described above. If the reason given in a sentence is a good and supportive one, write *convincing* in the space provided. If the reason given is actually just a restatement of the opinion, rewrite the sentence so that a supportive reason is given. The first one is done for you.

EXAMPLE: Visiting elderly people is a good thing to do because it is nice to care about old people.

Visiting elderly people is a good thing to do because these people will appreciate this caring and affection.

1. The Kitts' house was robbed because they left all their doors open.

   _____

   _____

2. It is time to take care of the mess in our front office because we should really keep it cleaner.

   _____

   _____

3. Everybody should own an automobile because cars are good to have.

   _____

   _____

4. People who sing on the bus are really annoying because they bother me a lot.

   _____

   _____

5. Pollution affects the daily lives of all of us because we are all affected by dirty air and water.

   _____

   _____

6. I enjoy being the center of attention at parties because I like people to pay a lot of attention to me.

   _____

   _____

7. The election this year was very close because both candidates received almost the same number of votes.

   _____

   _____

ANSWERS AND SOME REWRITTEN SENTENCES ARE ON PAGE 85.

4. *THE LAST THING TO REMEMBER ON AN ESSAY TEST IS TO READ THE QUESTION OR SITUATION SETUP VERY CAREFULLY.* It is important that you get all the information you need from the test item. Sometimes you may find clues that you did not see on your first reading of the question. A second or third reading of the material will assure you that you are prepared to answer the question.

In addition, you should know what you are being asked for before you begin to write. For example, look for statements like "Give two reasons." Knowing what you are expected to provide may save you time and effort. Sometimes a situation setup will not give any specific number, but instead give you two or three issues you will be expected to address. An example is given below.

> The nursing home where your mother lives is considering adopting a child-care program three afternoons a week. During these afternoons, children from local foster homes would come and be taught and entertained by the elderly.
>
> Some residents object to the program because they believe that the children will disrupt nonparticipants and that the children will not be adequately supervised.
>
> Do you think the nursing home should adopt the program? Why or why not? Write a paper to convince the residents of your point of view.

Can you see that your writing, regardless of what position you take, should address at least two issues? Since the situation setup clearly states two objections (disruption and inadequate supervision), you should discuss those issues in your writing. Of course, you are encouraged to discuss other pros and cons if you have enough time.

Exercise F: Persuasive Writing

 Choose <u>one</u> of the following situations and write a persuasive piece. Keep in mind what you have learned about good persuasive writing and make sure you use the correct format for the situation.

1. Your town is being considered for the site of a state fair. People from all over the state would come and participate in planned activities over the course of a whole summer. The people in your community must consider the pros and cons of the fair before they take a vote on it. Many people say the fair would bring new companies and growth to the community. Others think that the taxpayers will pay heavily and benefit little.

 Decide whether or not you would like your town to be the site of the state fair and write a piece defending your position. Give specific reasons for your decision.

2. You ordered a dollhouse kit from a Dreamchild, Inc., catalog on December 9 of last year. You sent a money order for $29.95, and as of today you have not received the kit or any communication from Dreamchild. You have decided that you no longer want the dollhouse kit, but you want your money back instead.

 Write a letter to the customer service department at Dreamchild. The address of the company is 99 Woodhollow Lane, Bangor, Maine 01111.

3. Your work supervisor is trying to put together a system that would cut down on theft in your company. Over the past several months, items ranging from plates of sheet metal to expensive blowtorches have been taken from the factory. There is controversy over whether the thieves are employees or outside people. Your supervisor has asked you to write down your opinion on the situation and what you think can be done to prevent these thefts.

 Put your writing in a job memo format. Remember to be specific about what you think the problem is and how you think it could be solved.

4. It has often been said that too much of the "good life" makes a person lazy and irresponsible. It is also a widely held belief that the more a person has, the more he wants. As one man put it, "Luxury makes a man so soft that it is hard to please him."

 Do you think that these beliefs are true? Why or why not? Give specific examples to support your opinion.

Continued

5. Lillian, a wife and mother of three children, gave a baby up for adoption when she was sixteen. She has never told her family about this part of her past. She has just been informed by the adoption agency that her child is anxious to meet his natural mother.

   Lillian wants to do what is right. She has no strong desire to meet her first child and does not want to give that child any hope that the two of them will have any kind of relationship. She is also afraid of what her family might think of her. On the other hand, she doesn't want the adopted child to suffer for something he has no control over. She believes that, in a way, the child has a right to know who his mother is.

   What would you advise Lillian to do? Remember that your job is to convince her of your point of view, so be specific and don't "beat around the bush."

6. Imagine that a rich relative or acquaintance is dying. He has announced that he wants to choose the one person to whom he will leave all his money. He has asked you and several other people to write down why you should receive the money rather than anyone else.

   Write your response, keeping in mind that you want to be as specific and convincing as possible.

7. On April 10 of this year you signed up for an exercise class at the local YMCA. The class cost $25 and was to run for eight weeks. After two classes, you became very dissatisfied with the class and the instructors. Not only was the class a half hour long instead of the promised one hour, but the instructors were rude and uncaring.

   Write a letter to the YMCA at 13410 Brooks Street in Tacoma, Washington 99888.

   In your letter, be sure to explain the situation clearly, tell the organization what you want it to do for you, give accurate and complete information, and use an acceptable format.

A GOOD PERSUASIVE PIECE OF WRITING BASED ON ONE OF THESE TOPICS IS GIVEN ON PAGE 85.

Chapter Checklist

An effective informative piece
- ☐ sticks to facts, not opinions
- ☐ answers who, what, when, how, and where
- ☐ presents facts clearly and is specific
- ☐ uses an appropriate format

An effective persuasive piece
- ☐ states opinion clearly in introduction
- ☐ supports point of view with good reasons
- ☐ summarizes opinion in closing paragraph
- ☐ is convincing to the reader

Exercise G: Informing and Persuading

 Give yourself approximately one half hour to write about <u>one</u> of the situations given below. This is what you would have to do in a test situation. Remember what you have learned in this chapter about good informative and persuasive writing. Three or four paragraphs should cover your topic. You may refer to the Chapter Checklist for help.

1. You were chosen from your department at work to attend a seminar about flexible hours in the workplace. You were asked to write up a memo to inform your fellow workers what the seminar was about. You have taken the following notes and now must write the memo.

   Remember that not all of the notes must be used in the memo. The name of your supervisor who requested the memo is Ms. Ellie Fedele, and the department you work for is the word processing pool.

   flexible working hours called "flex time"
       seminar's purpose is to tell pros and cons
   coffee and rolls provided
       employee must work 7 hours between hours of 7 A.M. and 11 P.M.
   can benefit both employer and employee in several ways
       employer has to pay less overtime since employees will be spread out over sixteen hours each day
   employee has time during day to take care of personal business since he is not restricted to 9 to 5 day
       good will between employee and employer
   I think the bad outweighs the good in flex time
       since salaried employees don't punch a clock, they have opportunity to cheat on hours worked
   system can be abused easily
       Kate Frost would probably work only 5 hours a day
   do employees who choose to work late at night get as much done as they would during regular hours?
       bills for overhead like electricity and heat are likely to be higher since used more hours

Continued

2. You ordered some tickets by mail to an auto show in the city. You were told that if you did not receive them by June 17, the show was sold out and you would be refunded the full ticket price.

   It is now July 27, the show begins today, and you have just received the tickets you ordered. Because you did not get the tickets by June 17, you assumed the show was sold out and that you would get a refund. You have made other plans and are no longer able to attend the show even though you have the tickets. You are upset about the way the ticket company handled the situation, and you definitely want a refund.

   The ticket company is TixMix and the company address is 908 Olympia Boulevard, St. Louis, Missouri 56565. You paid $12.00 for two tickets, and you paid with a money order, #32134. The ticket request was mailed on May 10 of this year.

   Write a letter to the customer service department of TixMix. Tell them what you would like the company to do for you, and make sure you give all the specific information they will need.

3. Sociologists are saying that there has been an increase in gang membership and gang activity in the 1980s. They say that the age of gang members now reaches as low as nine or ten years old and can go as high as thirty years old.

   Why do people join gangs? What is it about these groups that attracts so many people of so many different ages? Explain what you think the attraction is and give specific reasons for your statements.

*WRITING BASED ON ONE OF THESE
TOPICS IS ON PAGE 86.*

Answers

Exercise A

Here is a job memo based on the list of notes. Remember that yours may be a little different. Make sure you included all the information given in this memo and that you left out the irrelevant ideas. Also check to be sure you used the proper memo format.

To: Donna Mahan
From: Sam Peters
Re: Problems among floor clerks
Date: September 20, 1985

Ms. Mahan:

   I have thought about the major problems among the clerks, and I will briefly discuss them here. Basically, shifts are too long, and being on the floor for so long makes us irritable with customers. In addition, we are usually understaffed during sale times, and this also puts too much pressure on each clerk. Also, the fact that deliveries are made so late in the day makes it difficult for clerks to finish unpacking.

   Another problem is having too little cash in the drawer—something that has occurred September 1st, 9th, and 10th and several times every other month. This problem creates unnecessary trouble for clerks.

   Lastly, although we do have twenty-five clerks now, there is very little incentive to stay with the company. Most clerks feel that management should provide better reasons to stay with the outlet.

Exercise B

Below is a model informative business letter based on the situation given to you. Again, use this as a check for your work and make sure your letter has the same format and important features. You may have used different wording, but all of the specific information included should be the same.

January 12, 1985

Mr. Reginald Tierson
Personnel Department
Prontess Company
444 Lester Boulevard
Memphis, TN 21010

Dear Mr. Tierson:

   I have decided to accept the position of inventory clerk that you have offered me. I look forward to working at Prontess Company.

   As we agreed, I will be able to start work on February 15 of this year at a starting salary of $350 per week.

   I have also decided that I would like to participate in the Prontess group health insurance plan. I will be able to complete the paperwork whenever you would like.

Thank you again for your time and help, Mr. Tierson. I look forward to seeing you again on February 15.

Sincerely,

Donald Dowling

Donald Dowling

Exercise C

Here are some directions based on situation #2. Even if you chose this topic, your directions will obviously be very different. Were you as specific as the model given here? If you chose one of the other topics, you should check to be sure you gave all the specific facts your reader needs to understand you.

The name of the food warehouse where I shop is Wayside Mart, and the address is 335 Walnut Street. To get there from your house, take the #12 bus going west and get off at the Curtis Street stop. You will see an Arco gas station on your right.

Walk past the Arco station on Curtis until you get to Ash Hill Road, where you should turn left. So far, this is only about a five-minute walk. Walk only one block down Ash Hill, and you will come to Walnut Street. Take a right on Walnut, walk about three hundred yards, and Wayside is on your right.

Exercise D

This is a model letter of complaint based on the situation described to you. Check to be sure you used the same format and that you covered the same main points given in the model.

June 15, 1985

Customer Service Dept.
Naomi's Parlor
665 W. Burlington St.
Midtown, OH 52134

Dear Sir/Madam:

On June 9, I purchased two Naomi's pizzas from my local grocery store. When I opened them up, I found that one of them was covered with mold.

I was very upset to find this poor quality in a Naomi's Parlor product. I would like a refund, but I also would like to call your attention to the batch number, 03178, in case the whole batch has gone bad.

I paid $2.76 for the rotten pizza, and I would appreciate a prompt refund. I did not take this matter to my grocer because his standard of quality is very high, and this problem must have happened in your plant.

Thank you for your attention to this matter.

Sincerely yours,

Isabel Perkins

Isabel Perkins

Exercise E

Your rewritten reasons may be different from those given here. Just make sure you have given a good, supportive reason—not a simple restatement of the opinion.

1. *convincing*

2. It is time to take care of the mess in our front office **because it looks unprofessional to visitors.**

3. Everybody should own an automobile **because a car can be very handy in an emergency.**

4. People who sing on the bus are really annoying **because they interfere with my reading the newspaper.**

5. Pollution affects the everyday lives of all of us **because it is a threat to our health.**

6. I enjoy being the center of attention at parties **because my boyfriend gets jealous and buys me presents.**

7. The election this year was very close **because both candidates had similar viewpoints.**

Exercise F

These are models of persuasive writing based on choice #5. Both sides of the issue are represented here to emphasize the fact that persuasive writing can be good regardless of what point of view is taken. Notice how both essays discuss all issues and objections to both arguments. Regardless of which topic you picked, make sure you have all the elements of effective persuasive writing and that you address all the issues presented in the situation setup.

Essay #1

Lillian should refuse to meet her first-born son. Although the boy has rights, Lillian has some basic human rights as well. Everyone seems to favor the adopted child's wishes in this kind of situation, but we cannot ignore the mother's needs.

Lillian has chosen not to tell her family about this part of her past. This is her right. She should not feel it necessary to tell her husband and children about a private event that happened many years ago. By telling them, she risks losing their trust. By not telling them, she makes sure that neither she nor her family suffers.

If she did decide to risk her relationship with her family, who would gain anything? Some people think the adopted child would benefit. But Lillian is happy in her life now and honestly believes she wants to take no part in the future of this child. The child's hopes would be raised for nothing. He would feel a rejection that he did not have to feel.

Although some may feel that it is Lillian's son's right to meet her, we should look at who will really be better off as a result of the reunion. Lillian made a brave decision when she gave this child up for adoption, and she should not have to pay the price for it again. Her son should not have to bear the bitter rejection he will feel when he discovers that his mother's life is her own, not his.

Essay #2

I believe that Lillian should agree to meet with her son who was adopted as a baby. She brought the child into the world, and she should allow him to see his own flesh and blood. She has some reservations, but none are important compared to the wishes of her child.

This child was Lillian's family before she even met her husband and had his children. She should be honest about this part of her life and give her family the chance to accept this fact. Why are these children more important than her first child? If Lillian loves them, she will be teaching a wonderful lesson by showing them the importance of honesty and responsibility.

Lillian doesn't feel like she could actually take part in her adopted son's life. She doesn't want to get his hopes up for something she cannot or will not provide. However, when her son decided he wanted to meet his natural mother, he was aware of this risk. He is accepting this very real risk because he needs very badly to know his roots. How does Lillian know what this boy expects from her? Perhaps he just wants to know she exists.

This kind of situation presents risks for everyone involved. No one is denying this fact. However, we must stand up for the rights of the adopted boy, since he has had no choice in this situation whatsoever. We must take these risks in the hope that the innocent will gain something, however small.

Exercise G

Here is a job memo model based on choice #1. Make sure that you used a similar format and that you included only those ideas represented here. Some of the ideas on the list of notes were not relevant.

To: Ms. Ellie Fedele and Word Processing Pool

From: Rhonda Myers

Date: August 2, 1985

Re: Flexible hour seminar

The purpose of the seminar I attended last Monday was to discuss the pros and cons of "flex time." Flex time is the term used to refer to flexible working hours for employees. The basic format of flex time is that an employee must work any seven hours between the hours of 7 A.M. and 11 P.M. In the seminar, we learned both the benefits and the disadvantages of this system for both employer and employee.

One advantage of flex time to the employee is that he can use some of the traditional business hours to take care of personal needs, such as banking, doctor's appointments, etc. The advantage to the employer is that work can be going on constantly from 7 until 11. With regular hours, someone had to be paid overtime for this kind of time. Also, a great deal of goodwill can develop between employer and employee with this system, which is based on trust and mutual satisfaction of needs.

The flex time system does have some drawbacks. An employer is likely to notice a sharp increase in overhead costs since electricity and heat are needed for more hours of the day. Also, who can keep track of salaried employees' hours? Since they do not punch a clock, and are no longer accountable for the hours between nine and five o'clock, how does the employer know they are working seven hours a day? In addition, does the employee who works alone at night get as much accomplished as the one supervised from nine to five?

These are the main issues raised during the seminar. I will be happy to answer any questions and to pass on any new information I might get.

6. Revising Your Work

What Is Revision?

Your rough draft is like a ready-made garment that you buy right off the rack. The waist is too loose, the hem too low. The pants need to be altered to make them fit. Fixing a garment is a gradual process, requiring at least a couple of fittings to get everything just right. The same is true of turning your rough draft into a finished piece.

The first step in this "fitting" process is **revision**. You will take a new look at your piece of writing in order to decide what major changes it needs. At this point you will strengthen your piece to make it fit your audience and your purpose. Keep them both in mind as you decide what kinds of changes are needed to improve the overall ideas, organization, or form of your piece.

If you used a carefully prepared outline to write your first draft, you may not need to make major revisions. If you came up with new ideas while you were writing, that's fine. Just check to be sure your whole piece, including any parts that differ from your outline, still accomplishes your purpose.

It is important to make a distinction here between revising and editing. At this stage you don't have to worry about minor changes or editing. That will come in the second and possibly the third "fitting." Only then will you deal with fine-tuning word choice and with correcting grammar, capitalization, punctuation, and spelling.

Before you revise, it's a good idea to let your paragraph or piece sit for a while. If possible, leave your work alone for several hours. If that's not possible, even an hour will help. If you come back to something you've written after a break, you'll see it with a clearer, fresher eye.

When revising, first read the entire piece and then go over each individual paragraph within the piece. Why start with the whole piece instead of individual paragraphs? Because to start with individual paragraphs would be less efficient. For example, if you fixed an incomplete paragraph and then later decided not to include that paragraph, your efforts would have been wasted.

In addition, an overall reading of your piece will give you a sense of the whole—what you wrote and how you wrote it. This reading may also remind you of an important point you left out or an unimportant point that you really didn't want to emphasize.

Check Overall Structure

When working with a longer piece, you will want to start by checking its parts: introduction, body, and conclusion. Does each part do what it should?

Introductory Paragraph—introduces topic and sets stage for what will follow

Body Paragraphs—develop, explain, describe, prove what was presented in introduction

Concluding Paragraph—rewords introduction and summarizes body; gives piece finished feeling

If you find that any part is not doing its job, this is the time to fix it. For instance, something is missing from the short piece below.

PROBLEM:

Poor Introduction

My whole family was very disappointed with your television station and the hasty decision you made.

When you list something in the TV guide and then don't show the promised program, children can be hurt and confused. You owe it to them to make up for it somehow.

In addition, not only the kids, but also their mother and I, made special arrangements to be home for the program. We changed other plans we had made so that we could have a family evening together. I don't need to tell you that our night was ruined.

Continued

Continued from page 89

> Therefore, Mr. Winward, we are writing to register this complaint with you and all the directors of the ABC network. We hope this does not happen again, or we will be forced to turn to another station for good family entertainment.

In the writer's attempt to get his complaint out in the open, he has failed to tell the reader what the exact problem is in the introduction. He does not set the stage for what will be discussed in the body. From the body paragraphs you can get the idea that a family program was cancelled, but the reader should not have to guess about this. The writer should revise his introduction like this:

MODEL
Clear
Introduction

> My whole family was very disappointed with your television station and the hasty decision you made the night of January 10 of this year. Your network was supposed to show the children's special "Charlie Brown," but instead you showed the end of a football game!

It's the writer's responsibility to ensure that his writing includes everything necessary to make it understandable. A frustrated reader, one who has to struggle to find meaning, will often give up. When that happens, the writer's purpose isn't achieved, and all the work is wasted.

Once you know that the basic parts of your piece are providing the structural foundation and information they should, it's time to check other things. As you continue revising, check the piece as a whole first and then check individual paragraphs.

Principles of Clear Writing

There are four basic principles of clear writing you should check for:

1. Unity
2. Order
3. Emphasis
4. Completeness

We will discuss each of these principles in detail. As you revise your work, keep your audience and purpose in mind. No piece has unity, order, proper emphasis, and completeness if it does not suit your purpose.

1. UNITY MEANS EVERYTHING FITS TOGETHER TO CREATE ONE SINGLE IDEA OR EFFECT. Something that doesn't belong, something that's irrelevant, will distract from the single idea the writer wants to get across. It will be confusing and annoying to the reader. Check your writing for unity. If every paragraph, sentence, detail, and word helps make the main idea clear, the piece has unity.

This informative piece on eye contact lacks unity because there is one paragraph that does not support the unifying statement in the introduction. It is irrelevant and should be cut out. Read the piece and decide which paragraph does not fit.

PROBLEM:
Unity

Eye contact, just one aspect of body language, plays a big role in communication. Because of its powerful influence, there are different rules for eye contact in every place and situation. Observing the rules makes communication more comfortable. The important thing to know is how long to make eye contact.

For example, in an elevator, most of us look at everything except the eyes of other people. Because of the closeness, the contact is just too intense. On a bus you can look at others longer. At a party, when you're socializing, eye contact tends to last longer. And you may have noticed that in an auditorium the speaker can hold the eyes of the audience as long as he or she wants.

A strong handshake is also important. It expresses your genuine interest in another person. A weak handshake indicates disinterest or even rejection. A painful handshake indicates a desire to dominate.

Don't look at someone long enough to make him feel uncomfortable. You can cause embarrassment or anger if you stare too long. On the other hand, a friendly wink or glance might be just the thing to get your message across. Whether you're feeling friendly, shy, angry, or sexy, your eyes can say it for you.

The third paragraph about handshakes deals with an aspect of body language. However, the main idea for the piece, the idea introduced in the introduction and developed in the body paragraphs, is eye contact. Therefore, to have a unified piece, you would cut the third paragraph. Reread the piece, omitting the third paragraph, and see how much better everything holds together.

Unity is important in persuasive, narrative, and descriptive writing as well. You should be able to realize that an unrelated event in a story and an unrelated argument in a persuasive piece can ruin your whole purpose. Don't add more information just to lengthen your piece. Include only ideas and paragraphs that support your introduction.

2. ORDER MEANS THE LOGICAL ARRANGEMENT OF IDEAS. During revision you should decide whether your paragraphs are arranged in the most effective order for your audience and purpose. In pieces using sequence of events or space order, problems of order are usually easy to spot, particularly if you wrote from an outline and used transitions.

For other kinds of order, problems can be more subtle. In the piece below, all the paragraphs support the same idea. They have unity, but they are not arranged in order. Read the piece carefully to spot the problem.

PROBLEM:
Order

> I believe that my experience as a telephone customer service clerk indicates that I am both pleasant and capable of doing the job.
>
> My position as clerk with Sears customer service taught me the importance of good customer relations and attention to detail. I was responsible for over one hundred accounts, and I handled them professionally and efficiently. I hope you will look over my resumé and call to set up an interview.
>
> Therefore, I am writing in response to the ad labeled MBR 290 in last Sunday's Herald. The position was titled "Telephone Liaison."

Each paragraph in this letter is necessary and relevant. However, the order will confuse a reader. Before the writer starts discussing his experience, he should state the position he is applying for. It is confusing and frustrating for a reader to have to read two whole paragraphs before she can find out what the writer is discussing. Switching the placement of the first and last paragraphs, and taking out the transition *therefore*, will revise the piece so that it has correct order.

Exercise A: Revising for Unity and Order

 This exercise has two parts. The first is to revise the two pieces of writing below so that they have unity and correct order. To do this, simply put an *X* through any paragraph you feel does not fit (does not give unity to the piece). Then, if you feel that the paragraphs should be reordered, simply number them in the order you would like them in the final version.

For the second part of the exercise, go back and choose one of your own pieces from Chapter 3, 4, or 5. Revise this piece for unity and order.

1. I am writing to thank you for taking the time to talk to me last Thursday about the position of quality control specialist at J. Charron Manufacturing. I enjoyed the tour, and I was impressed by your facility and staff.

    If there is anything else I can give you to help convince you that I am the man for the job, Ms. Charron, just let me know. I look forward to hearing from you.

    Charron seems to be a friendly place to work, and I don't need to tell you how much I'd love to work in Albany. The city seems so clean, and I'm sure I could find an inexpensive but nice place to live with Ruby and the cat.

    As we discussed, I am very interested in moving from my present position of line checker to something with more responsibility. After meeting you and the other workers, I feel that J. Charron Manufacturing is the place for me.

2. If we all work together, the whole job can probably be finished by the end of May, and we will have beautifully clean streets and parks for the summer. Let's organize now.

    With the summer festival coming up, this is a good time to take care of cleaning up our neighborhood. As chairman of the Neighborhood Group, I propose that we organize now. Maybe we can even have some fun besides.

    If those on the west side of the street would be responsible for all streets and sidewalks, the east-siders can take care of Sturgis Park and Eaton Playground. There are enough families to get the work done on weekends.

    Let's take some time to see what our kids are learning in our neighborhood after-school group. Parents should get more involved than they have in the past. We could even organize a neighborhood parent advisory group.

THE REVISED WORK APPEARS ON PAGE 103.

3. REVISE YOUR WRITING FOR PROPER EMPHASIS. A piece has emphasis when the most important ideas stand out. Emphasis is achieved in two ways:

1. Position the most important idea at the beginning or the end of your paragraph or piece. Emphasis by position is particularly effective when your purpose is persuasive.

2. Write more detail about the most important idea. Just as the taller person tends to stand out in a crowd, the same is true in writing. A single, small detail is forgotten more easily than a richly detailed description or a fully developed explanation.

Often these two techniques are combined to make them even more effective. In addition, transitions can be added to make the emphasis even stronger. Look at the piece of writing below and see if you can tell what the writer's most important point is.

PROBLEM:
Emphasis

> I'll tell you why I've decided to take the nursing job at the hospital rather than at the clinic. My main reason is that the hospital offers more chance for advancement. Besides, it offers better pay and good medical benefits.
>
> The hours are shorter too. Instead of a regular forty-hour week, I'd be working just thirty hours. The clinic job would be from eight to five, five days a week. My hospital schedule will be just three ten-hour shifts: two days on, followed by a day off, then a night shift followed by four days off. That'll hardly seem like working at all. And there are even three weeks of vacation a year rather than two.

The second sentence states, "My main reason is that the hospital offers more chance for advancement," but that isn't really what stands out because most of the piece deals with differences in working time between two jobs. In fact, the writer devotes a whole paragraph to discussing job hours.

If the writer's main reason for her decision really is advancement opportunities, then the space devoted to hours should be cut down. In the same way, space devoted to advancement opportunities should be expanded. Read the revised piece below. Notice how the emphasis has been shifted.

> I'll tell you why I've decided to take the nursing job at the hospital rather than at the clinic. My main reason is that the hospital offers more chance for advancement. The director has indicated that, with my years of experience in different settings, he's willing to try me out as relief supervisor one night shift a week. If I do well, then he'll move me in to replace the day supervisor who's retiring next summer.
>
> Oh, there are other benefits with the hospital job, such as better pay, good medical benefits, shorter hours, and more vacation time, but I'm really excited about the opportunity to move into a supervisory position.

MODEL
Proper Emphasis

Now the piece emphasizes advancement opportunity by placing it first in the list of reasons, devoting more space to it, and briefly mentioning it again at the end. When you revise your writing, take time to think about your audience and purpose. Are you really getting your most important points across to your reader? What methods of emphasis will be most effective with your particular readers?

PARAGRAPH HIGHLIGHT #5

Once you've decided what paragraphs you will definitely keep in your longer piece of writing, it is time to look carefully at each individual paragraph. You'll have a chance later in the editing chapter to correct the punctuation, capitalization, and spelling in your work. In this Highlight, we will review the most common and serious error in a paragraph: the sentence fragment.

Sentence fragments (sentences that are not complete) are easy to overlook when revising your work because they seem to make sense in the context of a paragraph. Can you find any fragments in the paragraph below?

Clarella actually enjoys staying home and cooking and cleaning more than working in an office. She says she is the most liberated woman she knows. Because she is not afraid to say she loves being a housewife. She says she gets more pleasure from her husband's compliments about her cooking than she could get from a company car and a raise.

If you read the paragraph quickly, you may miss the fragment because it blends with the sentences around it to make sense. The fragment is the group of words beginning with *Because*. This fragment makes sense when read as if it were a part of the sentence before it.

Even though you can understand the writer's meaning, sentence fragments are incorrect and should be taken out of your paragraph. Combine such sentences like this:

She says she is the most liberated woman she knows because she is not afraid to say she loves being a housewife.

Watch out for sentence fragments that begin with words like *because, although, so that,* and other connecting words. Groups of words that begin with such words imply that a result, or a consequence, will follow. If this result is not included in the same sentence, the group of words is an impostor sentence. Practice detecting sentence fragments (impostors) in the next exercise.

Paragraph Highlight Exercise 5

The paragraphs below may contain sentence fragments. Rewrite each paragraph so that all sentences are complete. Do this by combining the fragments with other sentences or by adding ideas of your own.

1. While I am at work today, I'd like you to do the following things for me. Do the laundry that is in the hall basket. Because it has been sitting there for over two weeks. Next, please rearrange the TV room furniture. So that the baby cannot get near that glass table. If you get done with these two things. You can try making dinner with the recipes I left on the table.

2. Although the convict felt that he was not given a fair trial. He did not speak up. He feared that the crooks that he did business with would harm his family. If he said anything to anger them. Even though he was angry and hurt, Charles accepted the court's decision.

3. People who lie are the worst. They make mistakes and then try to cover them up with lies and half-truths. Just because they can't face other people's reactions. It will be a much better world, I think. When these dishonest people start facing facts.

4. The sharp-looking young man stood silently on the corner of Lake and Tanner. Acting as if he had not a care in the world. As a black car pulled up to the intersection. The man approached it and opened the back door. The car waited for a minute. Then the man got out and ran quickly into a nearby barber shop.

ANSWERS ARE ON PAGE 103.

4. THE LAST STEP IN THE REVISION PROCESS IS TO MAKE SURE YOUR PIECE IS COMPLETE. When paragraphs or pieces don't contain enough information to make the main idea interesting or clear, they are not complete. Remember, to be effective the body must adequately develop, explain, illustrate, or prove your main idea.

When deciding if your piece is complete, think about your purpose for writing. If you are telling a story, did you put in all the events needed to make your point? Did you include a beginning, a middle, and an end to the story? Most importantly, does your reader now have the whole picture you wanted him to get?

Completeness is also very important in persuasive writing. Think about what is needed to convince someone of your point of view. You should look at the situation from the other person's point of view and try to see how you might be able to overcome any objections. At the revision stage, be sure that you have addressed as many objections to your point of view as possible.

Leaving something out creates a hole in your argument and an excuse for your reader not to see your side of an issue. For example, let's look at the situation given below. Notice that the item gives you information about two points of view.

AN ESSAY TEST ITEM READS AS FOLLOWS:

"Your neighborhood has been having some trouble with crime and gangs, and the local city council is considering imposing a very early curfew hour on teenagers. The curfew law states that, regardless of the reason, all teenagers must be in their homes by seven o'clock at night.

"A large group of people object to this curfew. If a teen has a nighttime job, he is being asked to switch to a day shift. Many people think this is unfair and that it discriminates against the working youths, not the criminals. This group of people feels that increased police protection will be the solution that will rid the neighborhood of the problem.

"Write a piece explaining whether you agree or disagree with the curfew policy. Give good reasons for your point of view."

Here is how one writer addressed the issue:

> I believe that the curfew should be imposed. As a community, we are sick and tired of gangs and violence. We want a safe place for our kids to grow up.
>
> More police will not solve the problem. We already pay too much in taxes without adding to them by hiring more police. We already have plenty of policemen, and still crime persists.
>
> The police department can only do so much. This is our problem, and we must take care of it ourselves. The only way to stop this violence is to impose a curfew.

Were you persuaded by this person's argument? Or did you, like many other readers, say, "But what about the working kids? Isn't it unfair to them?" The problem with this piece of writing is one of incompleteness. The test question presents some people's objection to the curfew. They say it would hurt working youths. The author of this piece left a hole in his argument by not dealing with this concern.

To be persuasive about an issue, a writer must address the opposite point of view as well as his own opinion. Look at how another writer handled the test item. Notice that she uses the exact same point of view, introduction, and argument as the first writer did, but she adds additional reasons in the body paragraphs.

> I believe that the curfew should be imposed. As a community, we are sick and tired of gangs and violence. We want a safe place for our kids to grow up.
>
> More police will not solve the problem. We already pay too much in taxes without adding to them by hiring more police. We already have plenty of policemen, and still crime persists.
>
> The seven o'clock curfew is the only way to solve our problem. In this way, we will know that law-abiding youth are in their homes and that those who aren't in the home should be dealt with severely. How else can we isolate the good from the bad?
>
> Although this policy will force some working teens to change their schedules, the curfew is in their own best interests. Walking home from work at eleven at night is neither safe nor smart. Remember the three young people who, only last month, were attacked on their way home from work at night. Let's put some pressure on local businesses to give our kids morning, afternoon, and weekend hours. The problem of youth gangs and violence affects us all, and we must all sacrifice to solve it.

You may not agree with this person's point of view, but she did a much better job of persuading than the first one did. (1) She addressed the concern of some people for working youth. She argued that, although they will have to adjust, they will be better off with the curfew. (2) She gives evidence of this by pointing out the attack of the three youths on their way home from work. (3) She also adds an idea to help the working youth adjust—putting pressure on local businesses. This is good, complete, persuasive writing.

Exercise B: Revising for Emphasis and Completeness

Part 1

 Revise the letter to the editor below, paying close attention to emphasis and completeness. To help you do this, first answer the questions below.

1. The writer says in the introduction that he has three reasons for his opinion. Does he give all three reasons in his writing? If not, you will need to add a paragraph.

2. In the introduction, the writer tells you what his *most important* reason is. Does he make this reason really stand out in the body paragraphs? Does this reason appear either first or last, and does the writer put more detail and emphasis on this reason? If not, you will have to move the paragraph or add sentences.

I am writing to tell the readers of this newspaper that professional sports in America have gone too far. I believe this for three good reasons. One reason is that young people are being lured away from sticking with college sports by the big money offered to them. The second reason is that sports dominate every television channel during the weekend. But the most important reason is that these athletes make way too much money.

College athletes should be encouraged to stay in school and graduate. It is not surprising that these kids would rather make $50,000 a year than stay in school. But then, when their athletic careers are over, what do they have to fall back on with no college degree? Professional sports associations should have a responsibility to hire only college graduates for their teams.

Also, these athletes make a lot more money than they actually deserve. How about lowering ticket prices instead of paying multimillion-dollar salaries?

Part 2

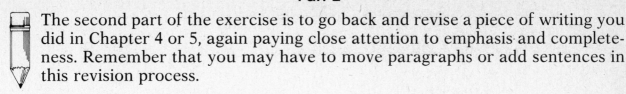 The second part of the exercise is to go back and revise a piece of writing you did in Chapter 4 or 5, again paying close attention to emphasis and completeness. Remember that you may have to move paragraphs or add sentences in this revision process.

THE REVISED LETTER IS ON PAGE 104.

Chapter Summary and Checklist

You have now learned the four basic things to watch out for as you revise your rough draft into a finished piece. Always keep your purpose in mind as you revise your work because no piece of writing is good unless you accomplish your purpose.

An effectively revised piece of writing

- ☐ has an introduction, body, and conclusion that accomplish their purposes
- ☐ has unity—one main idea expressed and supported
- ☐ uses correct order—ideas are arranged logically
- ☐ has proper emphasis—giving the most important points the most detail and placing them first or last
- ☐ is complete—addresses all the necessary issues in the topic so that purpose is accomplished

Exercise C: More Revising

Revise the following piece of writing, using the Chapter Checklist to help you check for unity, order, emphasis, and completeness. To help you go about this revision, first answer the questions below.

1. Does the introductory paragraph tell you what the piece will be about? Is there a unifying statement that tells you what the writer's purpose is? If not, you will need to add one. (**HINT:** Is it clear what "it" refers to in the first sentence?)

2. The introduction tells you all the things that went well on the trip. Are there any paragraphs that do not support this main idea of the piece? If so, you will need to take such paragraphs out.

3. In the introduction, the writer tells us the best thing about the trip. Is enough emphasis given to this idea? Since it is the most important, does it appear either first or last in the piece? If not, you will need to add more detail to this paragraph or move it so that it is properly emphasized.

The weather was perfect and the travel arrangements went well, but the best thing about it was how well I got along with my new stepchildren.

Hank had planned the trip perfectly. We left on Saturday afternoon, with the car laden with suitcases and coolers. Hank and I sat up front, and Sandy and Tyson spread out in back, so the rental car was plenty roomy. The directions we were given by AAA were excellent, and we arrived at the campground in plenty of time to set up the tents.

The good weather held up for us all weekend. It was warm and sunny all day, and the evenings were just cool enough to sit by the campfire. There was not a drop of rain the whole time. Our fears of two days being huddled in a tent luckily did not come true.

The worst thing that happened was that Hank had a headache and sore throat the whole time. He was coughing and sneezing all night, and he needed all of our coats and sweaters to keep warm while he slept. His health has ruined more than one weekend trip!

The best thing about the weekend away was getting to know Sandy and Tyson. We had a great time together.

THE REVISED PIECE IS ON PAGE 105.

Answers

Exercise A

1. I am writing to thank you for taking the time to talk to me last Thursday about the position of quality control specialist at J. Charron Manufacturing. I enjoyed the tour, and I was impressed by your facility and staff. (1)

   If there is anything else I can give you to help convince you that I am the man for the job, Ms. Charron, just let me know. (3) I look forward to hearing from you.

   Charron seems to be a friendly place to work, and I don't need to tell you how much I'd love to work in Albany. The city seems so clean, and I'm sure I could find an inexpensive but nice place to live with Ruby and the cat.

   As we discussed, I am very interested in moving from my present position of line checker to something with more responsibility. After meeting you and the (2) other workers, I feel that J. Charron Manufacturing is the place for me.

2. If we all work together, the whole job can probably be finished by the end of May, (3) and we will have beautifully clean streets and parks for the summer. Let's organize now.

   With the summer festival coming up, this is a good time to take care of cleaning (1) up our neighborhood. As chairman of the Neighborhood Group, I propose that we organize now. Maybe we can even have some fun besides.

   If those on the west side of the street would be responsible for all streets and sidewalks, the east-siders can take care of (2) Sturgis Park and Eaton Playground. There are enough families to get the work done on weekends.

   Let's take some time to see what our kids are learning in our neighborhood after-school group. Parents should get more involved than they have in the past. We could even organize a neighborhood parent advisory group.

Paragraph Highlight Exercise 5

1. While I am at work today, I'd like you to do the following things for me. Do the laundry that is in the hall basket because it has been sitting there for over two weeks. Next, please rearrange the TV room furniture so that the baby cannot get near that glass table. If you get done with these two things, you can try making dinner with the recipes I left on the table.

2. Although the convict felt that he was not given a fair trial, he did not speak up. He feared that the crooks that he did business with would harm his family if he said anything to anger them. Even though he was angry and hurt, Charles accepted the court's decision.

3. People who lie are the worst. They make mistakes and then try to cover them up with lies and half-truths just because they can't face other people's reactions. It will be a much better world, I think, when these dishonest people start facing facts.

4. The sharp-looking young man stood silently on the corner of Lake and Tanner, acting as if he had not a care in the world. As a black car pulled up to the intersection, the man approached it and opened the back door. The car waited for a minute. Then the man got out and ran quickly into a nearby barber shop.

Exercise B

Your revised piece may look a little different from the model below. However, make sure you added a paragraph about professional sports on television and put the most emphasis on the paragraph about high salaries. If you did these two things, your piece should be complete and properly emphasized.

I am writing to tell the readers of this newspaper that professional sports in America have gone too far. I believe this for three good reasons. One reason is that young people are being lured away from sticking with college sports by the big money offered to them. The second reason is that sports dominate every television channel during the weekend. But the most important reason is that these athletes make way too much money.

College athletes should be encouraged to stay in school and graduate. It is not surprising that these kids would rather make $50,000 a year than stay in school. But then, when their athletic careers are over, what do they have to fall back on with no college degree? Professional sports associations should have a responsibility to hire only college graduates for their teams.

Another example of professional sports going overboard is the amount of air time they monopolize on television. One used to be able to watch a good movie on Saturday afternoon or Sunday night. Now every channel is packed from morning to night with sports, sports, sports.

But by far, the most annoying aspect of professional sports is the fact that these athletes make a lot more money than they actually deserve. How about lowering ticket prices instead of paying multimillion-dollar salaries? Why should these young people with no education get paid hundreds of thousands of dollars for playing a sport once or twice a week? I believe we should go back to the days of amateur sporting events that aren't ruined by outrageously high stakes.

Exercise C

Your final piece may be different from what this writer came up with. You may have chosen a different ordering of ideas, and you may have added a different unifying statement. Be sure that you took out the paragraph about Hank's poor health since it does not support the unifying statement. Also be sure you put more emphasis on the paragraph about getting to know Sandy and Tyson because this was stated as the most important idea in the introduction.

Our weekend camping trip was a big success. The weather was perfect and the travel arrangements went well, but the best thing about it was how well I got along with my new stepchildren.

Hank had planned the trip perfectly. We left on Saturday afternoon, with the car laden with suitcases and coolers. Hank and I sat up front, and Sandy and Tyson spread out in back, so the rental car was plenty roomy. The directions we were given by AAA were excellent, and we arrived at the campground in plenty of time to set up the tents.

The good weather held up for us all weekend. It was warm and sunny all day, and the evenings were just cool enough to sit by the campfire. There was not a drop of rain the whole time. Our fears of two days being huddled in a tent luckily did not come true.

The best thing about the weekend away was getting to know Sandy and Tyson. This was the highlight of the whole trip. We had a great time together, and a lot of the resentment we had been feeling disappeared. The trip proved that we could make our new family work, and I was so glad I had agreed to try it!

7. Choosing Your Words

Why Focus on Word Choice?

Choosing words that say exactly what you want to say is like fine-tuning a radio or TV. It brings your ideas into sharp focus for your readers. And since no one else chooses words exactly the way you do, word choice is what makes your writing unique.

Typically, when you say someone does something "with style," you mean she makes something difficult seem smooth or easy. For example, you may admire the graceful skill of basketball players or pianists because of the apparent ease with which they dunk a ball or play a piece. But to master their skills, athletes and artists must learn to use the tools of their trade. Words are the writer's tools. This chapter provides four guidelines for word choice:

1. Be specific.
2. Be consistent.
3. Avoid repetition.
4. Avoid wordiness.

Be Specific

Think about the differences in meaning among these substitutes for *big:*

bulky	huge	enormous	massive	weighty
considerable	vast	immense	monstrous	
mighty	gigantic	colossal	impressive	

Which one of them would you choose if you were describing an ocean? What if you were describing a major decision?

Now look at these substitutes for *crazy:*

insane	mad	lunatic	unhinged	unbalanced
psychopathic	cracked	touched	moonstruck
scatterbrained	delirious	irrational	raving
eccentric	deranged		

Do you know someone who you think is crazy? Which of these words best describes that person? Think of a character on television or in a book or movie who is crazy. Pick a different word to describe that character.

It's easy to settle for tired, empty words like *nice* or *great,* but fresh, precise words will communicate better and make your writing interesting. For instance, for *nice,* if you mean *pleasing,* try *enjoyable* or *delightful.* If you mean *kind,* try *sympathetic* or *warmhearted.* Or, if by *great* you mean *good at something,* try *skillful* or *talented.* If you mean *impressive,* try *awesome.*

Sometimes it's hard to think of the exact word you need. When that happens, try looking in a dictionary or a thesaurus. First, think of a word that isn't quite right. If you look up that word in a dictionary, the dictionary will tell you how the word is used and give you some synonyms for it. (**Synonyms** are words that have almost the same meaning.) A **thesaurus**, which may be even more useful, gives lists of synonyms and related words for the word you look up. Often a dictionary or thesaurus will give you the word you're looking for. If not, you'll have lots of new ideas, and you may think of the right word yourself.

Your writing will be clearer if you use specific words and phrases to explain or describe. Your reader will <u>see</u> what you mean—actually picture it.

Exercise A: Choosing Specific Words

Read the paragraph below. Look at the underlined words. Choose more specific or more interesting words that could be used instead. If you wish, use a dictionary or thesaurus for ideas. Write the word or words you choose in the spaces below the paragraph. Then reread the paragraph with the new words to see how it sounds.

Working out <u>problems</u> with a co-worker can be almost as <u>hard</u> as trying to salvage a troubled marriage. The time we spend at work is usually about equal to our time at home, and personality differences can make a person <u>pretty</u> <u>upset</u> by the end of a day. We even tend to use the same kinds of attacks on co-workers as we do on our spouses—we ignore or <u>cut down</u> the person. But hardly ever do we try to "make up." If the problem gets too bad, a supervisor, foreman, or some other person is <u>asked</u> to help. But most often, just as in a marriage, <u>an answer</u> must be <u>found</u> by the two people themselves.

Original Word	Substitute Word
1. problems	_____
2. hard	_____
3. pretty	_____
4. upset	_____
5. cut down	_____
6. asked	_____
7. an answer	_____
8. found	_____

SOME MORE SPECIFIC SUBSTITUTE WORDS ARE ON PAGE 125.

Using Sensory Words to Strengthen Descriptive Writing

Specific words chosen with your purpose in mind make description more vivid and narrative more exciting. They also make information more interesting and persuasion more convincing.

In descriptive writing, strong sensory words create mental pictures. The choices are nearly limitless. Here are just a few of the possibilities:

sight—glistening, turquoise, transparent, velvety, smooth, rounded, square

taste—mouth-watering, tangy, bitter, sweet, salty, bland

touch—tingling, crusty, silky, sandpapery, oily, fluffy, crumbly, hot, sharp

smell—pungent, sweet, rancid, sour, spicy, moldy, musty

sound—thundering, screeching, earsplitting, whispering, crackling, sizzling, crunchy, rustling

Words that stimulate more than one of the five senses are especially effective. *Velvety*, for example, evokes the senses of touch and sight. *Spicy* evokes both taste and smell.

These sentences are not very descriptive.

This green salad is delicious.

John's new car is beautiful.

Notice how the use of sight, taste, sound, and touch words creates more complete pictures in the revised sentences below.

This spinach salad is crisp and tangy.

John's new car is a gorgeous, shiny red.

Putting Action into Narrative Writing

In a narrative piece, the emphasis is on the events themselves. Use action words (verbs) to make them exciting. Here are just a few examples of how you might choose action words. Which of these words would you choose to describe how you walk into a sleeping baby's room?

walk—ramble, shuffle, stride, scuttle, lope, tiptoe, strut, saunter

When you're in a bad mood, which of these best describes how you act?

complain—whine, pout, sulk, grumble, grouse, nag

Which word sounds official? Which one sounds sneaky?

look—stare, glare, glance, gaze, inspect, glimpse, peep

Think of the last scary movie you saw. Which of these words best describes what it did to you?

scare—frighten, horrify, startle, shock, spook, terrify, petrify

The narrative paragraph below seems lifeless.

PROBLEM:
No Specific Action Words

> Thirty seconds were left in the game. Tina got the rebound from Amy and threw it to Sherry. Sherry went down the court, but she fell. Chris saw the ball, came over, and took it. Then she made the long winning basket.

With stronger verbs, the paragraph can be brought to life.

MODEL
Word Choice

> Thirty seconds **remained** in the game. Tina **stole** the rebound from Amy and **passed** it to Sherry. Sherry **sprinted** down the court, but she **tripped**. Chris **spotted** the ball, **rushed** over, and **snatched** it. Then she **shot** the long winning basket.

You have just seen how descriptive action helps your narrative writing. Having the reader experience emotions also gives a narrative flavor. Read the sentence below.

Steve was nervous before his job interview.

The sentence merely tells us that Steve was nervous. We have no idea how Steve actually behaved. Now read this sentence.

Steve chewed his fingernails to the quick before his job interview.

Compare the sentence you just read to the original sentence about Steve. Do you see that the writer of the second sentence substituted a vivid picture phrase for *acted nervous*? This helps us to experience Steve's nervousness.

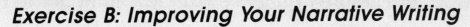

Exercise B: Improving Your Narrative Writing

Go back to the letter you wrote in Chapter 4, Exercise C, about your experience at a motel. See if you can replace words or phrases to make the events seem more real and alive.

SOME HINTS FOR IMPROVING THE LETTER ARE ON PAGE 125.

Clarifying Informative Writing through Word Choice

Informative writing is also strengthened if you use sensory details and strong action words. However, the most important feature of informative writing is clarity.

The paragraph below is vague. Would you be able to follow these instructions?

> Preheat the oven and put in the roast in the afternoon. Later, peel some carrots and cut them in pieces. Cook them while you make a salad from that stuff in the refrigerator drawer. Take out the roast at dinnertime.

PROBLEM:
No Specific Information

Now see how specific word choice can make these instructions very clear.

> Preheat the oven **to 400 degrees** and put in the roast **at 3:00 P.M. At 5:45**, peel **eight** carrots and cut them in **half-inch-thick** slices. **Steam** them **for 10 minutes** while you make a salad from the **lettuce, peppers, and onions** in the refrigerator drawer. Take out the roast at **6:15**.

MODEL
Specific Word Choice

Sometimes it's necessary to do a little research in order to locate information that is accurate, specific, and complete enough for your purpose. Knowledgeable people, at work or in your community, are usually willing to answer your questions. Often you can find out things you need to know by calling or visiting the public library.

Making Your Point with Positive and Negative Words

In persuasive writing, your purpose is to convince. Being convincing depends in part on using precise words that give the facts and on using interesting words to hold your reader's attention. Persuasion also depends on effective use of words with positive or negative meaning. Read the examples of positive and negative words below.

Positive	Negative
slender, svelte	skinny, thin
romantic	mushy
eccentric, individualist	crazy, oddball
colorful	gaudy
friendly, sociable	forward, pushy
inexpensive	cheap

Would you be likely to go to a movie that a friend told you was *romantic*? How about if you were told it was *mushy*?

Below is a paragraph that appeals to the reader's emotions in order to persuade. How does each word or phrase in dark type make you feel?

Incessant warfare between a husband and wife is far more **damaging** to children than the **clean break** of a divorce. No child should have to **endure day after day** of **gritted teeth** and **stony silence** or, **worse yet, shouting and screaming**. **Happy** parents in separate, **peaceful** households can provide children with **stability** and a **psychologically healthy atmosphere**.

What is the overall impact of the paragraph that is created by the words in dark type? Can you tell that the writer has a negative attitude about quarreling parents and positive feelings about peaceful divorce? Would the writer have been as convincing if she had used the word *trauma* in place of *clean break, disagreements* instead of *warfare*, or *recovering* instead of *happy*? Probably not. The writer has chosen words that describe divorce in a positive light and an unhappy marriage in a negative light.

In the exercise below, practice choosing words that persuade your reader.

Exercise C: Persuasive Words

Part 1

Fill in the blanks in the following advertisement with words or phrases that will convince the reader to buy the product.

This _____ new software program will take all the _____ out of your daily operations. It's _____ to learn and use. _____ technicians install the program and train you _____. You can also be sure that your _____ needs will be _____ when the program is tailored specifically for you.

A REWRITTEN VERSION OF THIS PARAGRAPH IS ON PAGE 125.

Part 2

Now fill in the blanks again, using words that will persuade the reader not to buy the software. Use words that give a negative impression.

This _____ new software program will take all the _____ out of your daily operations. It's _____ to learn and use. _____ technicians install the program and train you _____. You can also be sure that your _____ needs will be _____ when the program is tailored specifically for you.

A SECOND VERSION OF THIS PARAGRAPH IS ON PAGE 126.

Exercise D: Identifying and Replacing Weak Words

Read the paragraph below. Cross out words or phrases that are weak and write in words or phrases that are more specific, sensory, active, clear, or convincing.

We decided to eat out last night. It was evening when we entered a nice restaurant. A pleasant host put us at a pretty table set with clean linen and good china, glasses, and silver. The feeling of luxury was added to by quiet music and candlelight. A good waiter came to take our order. He brought a tasty soup. It was followed soon by tender sirloin tips, hot baked potatoes, fresh green salad, and homemade dinner rolls. For dessert we had delicious cake and coffee. It was a very nice evening.

SOME POSSIBLE WORD CHANGES FOR THIS PARAGRAPH ARE ON PAGE 126.

Be Consistent

In writing consistently, you are making sure that the words you choose all work together well and contribute to the purpose of your piece. You are making sure that your reader understands your main idea and purpose. Below is a narrative paragraph that lacks consistency. See if you can identify the problem.

PROBLEM:

Inconsistent Word Choice

Moving day was a real circus. My friend Richard comes over with a truck. First we will load the furniture. A leg broke off the sofa, and Richard set a chair on my foot. Then when we prop the front door open to get my big desk out, my cat ran out. You will see me hopping after her on one foot. When my mother arrives with iced tea and cookies, I was glad to take a break.

The story is confusing because of careless choice of verb tenses. Tenses are different forms of verbs that tell you whether the action is taking place in the past, present, or future. You're not quite sure whether these events already happened, are happening, or will happen. Writing that is inconsistent like this example can confuse and annoy your reader. Read the corrected version of the paragraph below.

> Moving day was a real circus. My friend Richard **came** over with a truck. First we **loaded** the furniture. A leg broke off the sofa, and Richard set a chair on my foot. Then when we **propped** the front door open to get my big desk out, my cat ran out. You **should have seen** me hopping after her on one foot. When my mother **arrived** with iced tea and cookies, I was glad to take a break.

MODEL
Consistent Word Choice

Now the sequence of events is clear, you know when the events took place, and you're not distracted by constant changes of tense. This is good, consistent writing.

Here is another example of inconsistent writing. As you read it, see if you can identify the problem. What words would you want to change if you revised the letter?

> To the Editor:
>
> As a parent, I would like to express my opinion about the Rocky Hill teachers' strike. Over the years, my kids have had super duper teachers. These teachers certainly merit more bucks. We know that experienced teachers all over the country are leaving their professions for jobs that pay better. If we don't treat these folks well here in Rocky Hill, we can't expect them to stick around. I urge the school board to raise teacher salaries immediately.
>
> Sincerely,
>
> Ron Waitts

PROBLEM:
Inconsistent Word Choice

The writer of this letter switches back and forth between formal and informal word choice. Part of it sounds like a casual conversation, and part of it sounds like a formal letter.

Now read the revised letter. Pay particular attention to the words in dark type. Notice that the informal language has been changed to more formal language.

MODEL
Consistent Word Choice

> To the Editor:
>
>   As a parent, I would like to express my opinion about the Rocky Hill teachers' strike. Over the years, my **children** have had **fine** teachers. These teachers certainly merit **a pay increase**. We know that experienced teachers all over the country are leaving their professions for jobs that pay better. If we don't treat **our teachers** well here in Rocky Hill, we can't expect them to **stay with us**. I urge the school board to raise teacher salaries immediately.
>
>   Sincerely,
>   Ron Waitts

Consistency is important to your reader. It makes your writing clear, smooth, and more convincing. To check for consistency in the exercise that follows, ask yourself:

- Are sensory words consistent with how you want to describe something?
- Are mood, style, and tone consistent throughout?
- Are verb tenses consistent with each other?
- Do positive and negative words create a single effect?

Exercise E: Making Wording Consistent

 The paragraph below contains inconsistencies in style and tone. The writer switches back and forth between formal and informal in choosing her words. Revise the paragraph by replacing the informal language so that the paragraph is consistently formal.

The president finally got ticked off and told us department heads to get our act together. He stated clearly that he expected us to execute our responsibilities promptly and efficiently. We all knew darn well that if we didn't get cracking, we'd find ourselves out on our rear ends. Some of us were quite relieved to see Mr. Washington finally put his foot down. We had long been aware that administrative procedures had fallen apart at the expense of production and sales.

A CONSISTENT PARAGRAPH CAN BE FOUND ON PAGE 126.

PARAGRAPH HIGHLIGHT #6

A common source of confusion for your reader is misplacement of words or phrases. The location of just one word in a sentence can affect the sentence's meaning. Read the sentences below. Notice how the meaning changes as the underlined words are moved.

We all do the work together.
We do all the work together.

Only he ate the Greek salad.
He only ate the Greek salad.
He ate only the Greek salad.
He ate the only Greek salad.

Well, he never writes a letter.
He never writes a letter well.

Sometimes misplacement of a word or phrase can lead to funny, impossible, or nonsense statements. Read the incorrect sentences below. Think about exactly what each sentence says. Then read the corrections to see what the writer really intended to say.

Incorrect: We were not bothered by the bugs with insect repellent.
Correct: With insect repellent, we were not bothered by the bugs.

The first sentence sounds like the bugs have the insect repellent.

What is the mistaken idea in each of the following sentences?

Incorrect: Joanna studied the photo hanging on the wall carefully.

Correct: Joanna carefully studied the photo hanging on the wall.

Incorrect: I have visited the place where Steve is buried many times.

Correct: Many times I have visited the place where Steve is buried.

A second source of confusion is missing words. Again, look at the incorrect sentences and then the corrected ones to see the problem and how it was solved.

Incorrect: When writing, it's hard to remember all the comma rules.

(Who or what is writing?)

Correct: When I'm writing, it's hard to remember all the comma rules.

Incorrect: Swimming at the beach, Mary's Sony Walkman was stolen.

(Have you ever seen a Sony Walkman swim?)

Correct: When she was swimming at the beach, Mary's Sony Walkman was stolen.

The confusion in these pairs of sentences was created because the writer left out the person or persons needed to perform the action. When you're writing, it's easy to assume that everything is clear to the reader. But it's necessary to check whether you have actually said who's performing each action.

In the exercise that follows, practice clearing up confusion caused by misplaced or missing words and phrases. Think about what the writer is really trying to say. Remember to place describing words and phrases as close as possible to what they describe. Also be sure that the reader can tell who is performing each action.

Paragraph Highlight Exercise 6

Rewrite the following paragraph so that there is no confusion caused by misplaced or missing words or phrases.

Traveling at night, the heavy traffic became too tiring to go farther. We came to a diner in a small town that was still open. My partner Jack climbed down from the truck already wearing a coat. Waiting for me, his impatience got the better of him. He entered the diner and seated himself at a table with a glance around the room. Finally entering, my heart stopped when I saw the waitress approaching Jack. I had seen her before.

A REWRITTEN PARAGRAPH APPEARS ON PAGE 127.

Avoid Repetition

It's easy, especially when you're writing a first draft, to be repetitious. Repetition is occasionally needed to clarify or reinforce a point, as in the summary part of a conclusion. However, repetition can cloud your meaning and make your readers feel like you're "talking down" to them. In general, you should avoid repetition.

One of the most common repetition problems occurs when you use the same subject and the same verb over and over. When you're checking your writing for word choice, be on the lookout for repetitions like the ones in the paragraph below.

PROBLEM:
Repetition

> With a home computer, you can do more things all the time. You can study anything from typing to Japanese. You can play simulation games. They can challenge you to operate a business at a profit or cross the Oregon Trail. You can play video games like Ms. Pac Man. And computers can help with time-consuming chores. You can do inventories, checkbook balancing, taxes, or recipe filing. Your computer can even pay bills and take care of banking. Or you can use the word processor and make changes right on the screen. You can correct spelling and print multiple copies.

The verb *can*, especially with the subject *you*, is repeated throughout the paragraph. Now read another version of the paragraph. Not every *you can* has been eliminated, but most have.

MODEL
Varied Word Choice

> **A home computer allows you to do** more things all the time. You can study anything from typing to Japanese. **Simulation games challenge you** to operate a business at a profit or cross the Oregon Trail. **If fun is your thing, play** video games like Ms. Pac Man. **Computers help** with time-consuming chores like inventories, checkbook balancing, tax preparation, and filing recipes. Your computer can even pay bills and take care of banking. **Some people** use the word processor more than anything else, **making changes** and correcting spelling right on the screen **and then printing** multiple copies.

Another kind of repetition occurs when the same describing word or phrase is repeated several times in a passage. Here's an example.

PROBLEM:
Repetition

> Kathryn Ostrosky is the best worker I have. She's the most organized and the most efficient, and she is very prompt and never sick. She's very courteous and is great at getting along with her co-workers. Kathryn is also very eager to learn new skills and is great at getting things right the first time. I am most pleased to recommend her for a promotion. She will be a great success in whatever she does, although I will be very sorry to lose her.

Most, very, and *great* are all repeated more than once in the paragraph. Such repetition is distracting. It prevents the reader from concentrating on the important things the writer is saying about Kathryn. Extreme or absolute words like *great, very, quite, best, worst, most, always,* and *never* should be used sparingly and only when they are true. They lose their impact if repeated too often. Either substitute more precise words or eliminate them. The repetitions in the paragraph about Kathryn Ostrosky have been eliminated in the version below.

Kathryn Ostrosky is the best worker I have. She's the most organized and efficient, and **she is prompt** and never sick. She's courteous and **gets along well** with her co-workers. Kathryn is also eager to learn new skills and **is likely to get** things right the first time. **I am pleased** to recommend her for a promotion. She will **be successful** in whatever she does, although I will **certainly be sorry** to lose her.

MODEL
Varied Word Choice

If you may find yourself repeating a "pet" word or phrase that's different from the ones above, the same principles still apply: use sparingly, use substitutes, or leave out entirely. The exercise below provides you with practice in eliminating repetitions.

Exercise F: Eliminating Repetition

Rewrite the paragraph below to eliminate unnecessary repetition. You will probably need to add and delete words, rearrange some of the ideas, and combine sentences.

On payday, Jan and Rick had their first argument since they were married two months ago. Their first argument was about Jan's paycheck. Rick simply assumed that Jan's paycheck would go into his checking account. He simply assumed this without talking to Jan. He assumed Jan's paycheck would go into his account because that was how his parents handled their money. He assumed all married couples handled their money like his parents. He couldn't understand why Jan wouldn't want her paycheck going into his account.

THE REWRITTEN PARAGRAPH IS ON PAGE 127.

Avoid Wordiness

Wordiness means using more words than necessary to say something. It also means using different words but saying the same thing twice. For example, *at the present time* means the same thing as *present* or *now*. *About 3:00 P.M.* is preferable to *in the afternoon at about 3:00 P.M.* Instead of helping readers, extra words tend to make ideas harder to grasp. They act like fog, clouding the picture and lessening the impact of the writer's ideas. Read the pairs of sentences below. In each pair, the first sentence either uses more words than necessary or repeats something with different words. The second sentence has been rewritten without unnecessary words.

> You don't have to refer back to past history to see examples of corruption.
> You don't have to **refer to history** to see examples of corruption.

> We decided at that point in time to call the police.
> We decided **at that point** to call the police.

> My best friend, she's a very unusual person.
> My best friend **is** a very unusual person.

> He is a man who can be depended upon to do what he says he will do.
> **He can** be depended on to do what **he says**.

Be on the lookout for wordiness in your writing. When you cut out the "fog," your writing will be clear and more powerful.

Now try eliminating words in the exercise below.

Exercise G: Avoiding Wordiness

Part 1

Rewrite the following sentences to eliminate wordiness.

1. I have been waiting to see the doctor for a long period of time.

2. He could spit a distance of 100 feet.

3. The absolutely necessary essentials of a good love relationship are humor and patience.

4. Enclosed herewith please find two tickets to the Bears game.

5. Please remember the fact that my name is not "Honey."

6. They are engaged in taking a survey of their customers.

7. You know it's your turn to go when the color of the light is green.

8. I will keep these papers until such time as you can come in to sign them.

9. The Easter eggs are eight in number.

Part 2

Now cross out all unnecessary words in the following piece.

My grandmother was quite a daring adventurous woman for her day in the 1920s. She went to college in her hometown where she grew up to learn to be a teacher. After she graduated, her first job out of college was in Billings, Montana, so she packed up, left her family and friends behind, and headed west to teach in Billings.

After a couple of years of teaching, she decided she had had enough of that quiet life that didn't offer much excitement. She decided to follow her natural talents as an artist and go to art school in Chicago. So, by herself, she moved to the big city on her own to live.

During the period of time she lived in Chicago, she dated several different men, one of whom eventually one day became my grandfather, her husband. She finally settled down with him at last and got married at age 27. My grandmother, she always will tell us female women in my family what a mistake her daughters made and how much of their young youth they missed by getting married to their husbands immediately right after graduating from college.

ANSWERS AND AN IMPROVED PIECE ARE ON PAGE 127.

Following the principles of word choice will do a lot to give your writing vigor, clarity, and grace. Sometimes you may encounter a rough spot you just can't smooth out. If you're not sure your wording is clear, share your piece with a friend or co-worker. Another person's opinion and suggestions may be just what you need to add the final touches. Use the following Chapter Checklist as you revise one of your own pieces of writing in Exercise H.

Chapter Checklist

Writing that uses good word choice

☐ has words that fit your purpose
☐ uses specific rather than general words
☐ is consistent in tone, style, and tense
☐ has no misplaced or omitted words
☐ does not repeat words and phrases unnecessarily
☐ is not wordy

Exercise H: Fine-Tuning Your Writing through Word Choice

Return to one of your own pieces of writing from Chapter 4 or 5. Use the Chapter Checklist as you make changes that will improve your piece.

Answers

Exercise A

You may have come up with different substitute words. Just make sure yours are specific and full of life, not dull and general.

Original Word	Substitute Word
1. problems	conflicts
2. hard	tough
3. pretty	rather
4. upset	irritated
5. cut down	insult
6. asked	requested
7. an answer	a solution
8. found	discovered

Exercise B

Look at your revisions. Did you use action words to make the events come alive? Read through your piece to see which verbs are not action words. Can you change them? What about the ones that are action words? Can you make them more interesting? Make sure each sentence makes you picture an event or feel a feeling.

For example, you could have said you were **forced** to wait thirty minutes for the desk clerk and that the porter **destroyed** the lock on your luggage. You could have **requested** of the manager that he **reduce** the heat.

Exercise C

The models below are meant only as guides for you to check your work against. In Part 1, did you use positive words that make the product look good to the reader? In Part 2, did you fill in the blanks with words that have a negative feeling?

Part 1

This **useful** new software program will take all the **problems** out of your daily operations. It's **simple** to learn and use. **Qualified** technicians install the program and train you **instantly**. You can also be sure that your **important** needs will be **accommodated** when the program is tailored specifically for you.

Part 2

This **worthless** new software program will take all the **pleasure** out of your daily operations. It's **impossible** to learn and use. **Unprepared** technicians install the program and train you **haphazardly**. You can also be sure that your **important** needs will be **ignored** when the program is tailored specifically for you.

Exercise D

We decided to ~~eat~~ *dine* out last night. It was ~~evening~~ *dusk* when we entered ~~a nice~~ *an elegant* restaurant. A ~~pleasant~~ *cordial* host ~~put~~ *seated* us at a ~~pretty~~ *beautiful* table set with clean linen and ~~good~~ *sparkling* china, glasses, and silver. The feeling of luxury was ~~added to~~ *enhanced* by ~~quiet~~ *romantic* music and candlelight. A ~~good~~ *competent* waiter ~~came~~ *arrived* to take our order. He brought a ~~tasty~~ *creamy* soup. It was followed ~~soon~~ *promptly* by tender sirloin tips, ~~hot~~ *steaming* baked potatoes, ~~fresh~~ *crisp* green salad, and home-made ~~dinner rolls~~ *biscuits*. For dessert we had ~~delicious~~ *rich* cake and coffee. It was a ~~very nice~~ *tremendous* evening.

Exercise E

The model below has a consistent tone throughout. Notice how all the informal expressions have been replaced with words and phrases that are appropriate to the rest of the piece.

The president finally got **angry** and told us department heads to **improve performance**. He stated clearly that he expected us to execute our responsibilities promptly and efficiently. We all knew **very** well that if we didn't **increase productivity**, we'd **lose our positions**. Some of us were quite relieved to see Mr. Washington finally **assert himself**. We had long been aware that administrative procedures had **deteriorated** at the expense of production and sales.

Paragraph Highlight Exercise 6

Notice that in this model all describing words and phrases are as close as possible to the words they describe. Also notice how the writer has added words and phrases to make her meaning clearer to the reader.

Traveling at night, **we found that** the heavy traffic became too tiring to go farther. We came to a diner **that was still open** in a small town. **Already wearing a coat**, my partner Jack climbed down from the truck. **As he waited** for me, his impatience got the better of him. He entered the diner and, **with a glance around the room**, seated himself at a table. **As I finally entered**, my heart stopped when I saw the waitress approaching Jack. I had seen her before.

Exercise F

The model below is an example of how you can get rid of repetitions in your writing. Were you able to combine sentences and use synonyms to get rid of the repetitions?

On payday, Jan and Rick had their first argument since they were married two months ago. The **disagreement** was about Jan's paycheck. **Without talking to his wife**, Rick simply assumed that it would go into his checking account because that was how his parents handled their money. **He thought that was how** all married couples managed their money. He couldn't understand why Jan **wanted things to be different**.

Exercise G

Part 1

1. I have been waiting to see the doctor **for a long time**.
2. He could spit **100 feet**.
3. The **essentials** of a good love relationship are humor and patience.
4. **Enclosed are** two tickets to the Bears game.
5. Please remember **that** my name is not "Honey."
6. They **are** taking a survey of their customers.
7. You know it's your turn when **the light is green**.
8. I will keep these papers **until** you can come in to sign them.
9. **There are eight** Easter eggs.

Part 2

The model piece below is no longer wordy and repetitive. Make sure you got rid of unnecessary words and phrases from your piece.

My grandmother was quite a daring ~~adventurous~~ woman for her day in the 1920s. She went to college in her hometown ~~where she grew up~~ to learn to be a teacher. After she graduated, her first job ~~out of college~~ was in Billings, Montana, so she packed up, left her family and friends behind, and headed west to teach ~~in Billings~~.

After a couple of years of teaching, she decided she had had enough of that quiet life ~~that didn't offer much excitement~~. She decided to follow her natural talents ~~as an artist~~ and go to art school in Chicago. So, ~~by herself,~~ she moved to the big city on her own to live.

During the ~~period of~~ time she lived in Chicago, she dated several ~~different~~ men, one of whom ~~eventually~~ became my grandfather, her husband. She finally settled down with him ~~at last~~ and got married at age 27. My grandmother, ~~she~~ always will tell us ~~female~~ women in my family what a mistake her daughters made and how much of their ~~young~~ youth they missed by getting married ~~to their husbands~~ immediately ~~right~~ after graduating from college.

8. Editing Your Work

What's the Purpose of Editing?

After revising the first draft and fine-tuning the wording of a piece of writing, the next step is editing. **Editing** means making sure that you've followed the rules for using capital letters and punctuation and that your spelling and grammar are correct. This chapter will go into the aspects of grammar that affect basic punctuation rules, but it will not cover every grammar issue. You might want to get a grammar handbook that you can refer to when questions come up.

Editing is important for two reasons. The first is image. First impressions do influence how other people respond to you and to your writing. You don't want your readers to be distracted from your message because of careless handling of details.

The second reason for editing is that it helps your readers. If your writing is filled with errors, even small ones (such as misspelled words or a few missing or misused capitals and punctuation marks), they may do more than just distract your readers from your ideas. They may actually cause your readers to misunderstand you or become so confused that they give up. After careful preparation of a piece of writing, it would be a shame to let small errors interfere with effective communication.

What Does Editing Look Like?

When you edit, you should cross out things you want to remove and write in corrections. Be sure that your markings are big enough and dark enough that you won't miss them later, especially small things like periods and commas. If you want to insert something, put a caret (∧) in the line where it goes. Then write what you want to insert above the line.

Here is an example of an edited piece of writing:

I always thought that what my wife ~~don't~~ know *didn't* ∧ wouldn't

hurt her. My problem is that she always finds out the things

I think she'll never know∧ ~~and~~

Check Your Capitalization

First Word in a Sentence

The first word in a sentence is always capitalized. This rule also applies to quotations within sentences when the quotation is a complete sentence.

My husband is usually in a bad mood when we do our income taxes.

Is the zoo northwest of here?

Ms. Boling said, "**Congratulations**, Carl, you're the new buyer for the sportswear department."

"**Jack** was born on Mother's Day," said John. "**He** is our first child."

Proper Nouns

Proper nouns are always capitalized. Examples of proper nouns are people's names and names of places, such as cities or countries. In addition, you can think of the word *I*, which is always capitalized, as being a proper noun. *I* is also capitalized when it is part of a contraction such as *I'm* for *I am*, *I've* for *I have*, *I'll* for *I will*, *I'd* for *I would*, etc.

Could **I** get **Katherine** to help me edit my letters?

Yes, **I'm** going to **Arkansas** tomorrow.

Abbreviations and Initials

A letter that stands for an entire word is always capitalized. For example, *U.S.S.R.* stands for *Union of Soviet Socialist Republics*. If an abbreviation has more than one letter, the first letter is always capitalized. For example, *Jr.* stands for *Junior*.

An initial that is part of someone's name is always capitalized, as in John **D.** Rockefeller or **J. P.** Stevens.

General vs. Specific

You can usually tell if a word should be capitalized by figuring out if it is used in a general or a specific way in the sentence. A word should be capitalized only if it identifies the specific name of a person, place, or thing. On the next few pages are some categories of things that you might need to capitalize.

1. CAPITALIZE THE NAMES AND TITLES OF SPECIFIC PEOPLE. Some words can be used either as general words or as titles. Examine how a word is used in a particular sentence to decide whether it is being used in a general way (My **uncle** lives in Louisville) or as a specific person's name or title (My **Uncle George** lives in Louisville).

One of the most common capitalization errors is capitalizing occupations. Be sure not to capitalize unless you're using the word as part of a person's title or name.

Incorrect: Mrs. Kelly is the **Nurse** on the case.

Correct: Mrs. Kelly is the **nurse** on the case.

General	Specific Title
doctor	Doctor Sydnam
president	President Kennedy
representative	Representative Ashmore

In the 1985 election I voted for Robert Goldberg for **mayor**. I am sure he'll do a better job than **Mayor Elliot**.

The **officer** who investigated the case and wrote the report was **Officer Mirk**.

2. CAPITALIZE THE NAMES OF SPECIFIC PLACES, ORGANIZATIONS, BUSINESSES, AND GOVERNMENT BODIES.

General words for these are not capitalized except when they are used as a part of a specific name. Once again, look at the sentence to decide whether a word is being used in a general way (We crossed the **river**) or as part of a specific name (We crossed the **Tennessee River**).

Capitalize terms, such as nationalities and races, that are based on the names of geographic places. Sometimes these specific names are used to describe nonspecific things (such as *Chinese food*). In this case, do not capitalize the word being described (*food*).

Do not capitalize words like *north*, *south*, *east*, and *west* when they are used as a direction or descriptive term. Only capitalize them when they are part of the name of a place, an organization, or a geographic region.

General	Specific
geographic region	the Middle East, the Southern Hemisphere
street, highway	Washington Street, Kennedy Highway
nationalities, languages, races	Spanish, Korean, Afro-American
city council, court	Knoxville City Council, Supreme Court
company, corporation	General Motors Corporation
department, agency	Department of Energy

I learned to speak **French** from my **German** lover.

One of the **departments** in the company is involved in a dispute with the **Department of Labor**.

The **east** bank of the **East River** is lovely in that area.

My brother always travels **west** for the summer.

3. CAPITALIZE THE NAMES OF HISTORICAL EVENTS OR PERIODS, SPECIAL EVENTS, AND CALENDAR ITEMS.

General	Specific
historical events or periods	Vietnam War, Victorian Era
special events	World Series, Democratic Convention
calendar items	Sunday, March, Labor Day

Do not capitalize the names of the seasons: *spring, summer, winter, fall, autumn.*

> The **Great Depression** was the worst case of economic **depression** this country has ever seen.

> A good **day** to have a barbecue would be **Memorial Day**.

> The **Provincetown Fine Arts Festival** is held in early August. The **festival** features many local artists.

4. CAPITALIZE SPECIFIC TITLES OF THINGS LIKE BOOKS, ARTICLES, MAGAZINES, MOVIES, AND SHOWS. In a title, capitalize all the words except articles (*a, an,* and *the*) and prepositions (such as *with, on, in, to,* and *for*). Also, the first and last words in a title are always capitalized.

General	Specific
book	How to Insulate Your House
newspaper	Los Angeles Times
magazine	Sports Illustrated
poem	"The Raven"
article	"A Diet for a Better Body"
television show	"All in the Family"

> My heart went out to the teenage boy when I saw the movie **Ordinary People**.

> Have you seen the latest issue of **Cosmopolitan**? This month, the whole magazine is about sex.

> Jane Austen's book **Pride and Prejudice** was written before 1800, but lots of people still read it and love it today.

Exercise A: Editing for Capitalization

There are capitalization errors of all kinds in this paragraph. Cross out the errors and write in your corrections.

Super bowl sunday has got to be the most controversial event of the year in my family. You'd think my children were the Football Players. My Son and daughter always have to choose opposite sides. When the Miami dolphins played the San Francisco 49ers, they argued for days about which Team should win. They even wrote an article for their high school paper, "Brother And Sister divide Family on Super Bowl Question." They interviewed their Grandfather in Miami and their aunt Sarah in san Francisco by phone for the article.

THE EDITED PARAGRAPH IS ON PAGE 156.

Check Your Punctuation

Imagine driving down a busy street with no center lines, no traffic lights, no traffic signs. What do you do when you get to an intersection? How do you find your way in new territory? Reading sentences without commas, periods, question marks, and exclamation marks is as hard as driving without signs or lights.

Punctuating the End of a Sentence

1. A TYPICAL STATEMENT ENDS WITH A PERIOD.

I voted for Ronald Reagan.

A study revealed a link between coffee drinking and cancer.

2. A QUESTION ENDS WITH A QUESTION MARK.

Whom did you vote for?

Why can't he keep his opinions to himself?

Be careful not to put a question mark at the end of an indirect question. An indirect question may use a question word such as *why* or *asked* but is actually a statement.

Incorrect: I asked if she would go to the circus with me?

This statement tells you that a question has been asked.

Correct: I asked if she would go to the circus with me.

3. A COMMAND OR AN INSTRUCTION ENDS WITH A PERIOD.

Do not exit.

Send this by Express Mail tomorrow.

4. TO SHOW EMOTION OR EMPHASIS, END A STATEMENT WITH AN EXCLAMATION POINT.

That is a great idea!

Things are getting so expensive!

Using Commas in Sentences

You are about to learn a lot about using commas. Be careful to use them only when you really need them. If you have any doubt about whether you need a comma, be sure you are actually following one of the comma rules before you use one. If you can't find a reason for using a comma, don't use one. Extra punctuation is very confusing to your reader.

1. USE A COMMA BEFORE THE CONNECTING WORDS AND, BUT, OR, NOR, FOR, AND YET WHEN THEY JOIN TWO COMPLETE THOUGHTS.

These words are commonly used to join choppy sentences together and make writing smoother.

Mario lives on the eleventh floor.

He works in the restaurant on the ground floor.

These two sentences can be combined using the connecting word *and* and a comma, like this:

Mario lives on the eleventh floor, **and** he works in the restaurant on the ground floor.

You get the job done on time, **or** I'll replace you with someone who can.

Be sure that you really are joining two sentences. People often make the mistake of using a comma wherever there is an *and* in the sentence. Do not use a comma unless each part is a complete thought.

Incorrect: I will take business courses at the community college during the day, and work at the Wharf Tavern at night.

Correct: I will take business courses at the community college during the day and work at the Wharf Tavern at night.

Notice that, in the incorrect version above, *and work at the Wharf Tavern at night* is not a complete thought—it can't stand by itself as a sentence.

Also, don't join two sentences with a comma and forget to put in a joining word.

Incorrect: The plant was about to die, I gave it to my sister.

Correct: The plant was about to die, so I gave it to my sister.

2. WHEN A RELATED IDEA COMES BEFORE A COMPLETE THOUGHT, PUT A COMMA AFTER THE RELATED IDEA. Many sentences consist of a related idea and a complete thought. A related idea has a subject and a verb, but it could not stand on its own as a complete sentence. Related ideas begin with words like *if, because, when, where, before, after,* and *although.* A related idea could always come either before or after a complete thought in a sentence.

If you want me to, I'll stay here.

Notice that, in the sentence above, *If you want me to* is not a complete thought. However, it does have a subject, *you,* and a verb, *want.* It is followed by a comma.

Because Dave wants to use this room, I'll move next door.

Although I love my mother, I can't live with her anymore.

Whenever I get a chance, I read the newspaper.

Before you leave in the morning, make sure the stove is turned off.

Be careful not to use a comma if the related idea comes <u>after</u> the complete thought.

Incorrect: I'm not allowed to eat salt, because my blood pressure is too high.

Correct: I'm not allowed to eat salt because my blood pressure is too high.

Exercise B: Editing for Punctuation

 In the following excerpts from a church newsletter, there are six punctuation errors like the ones you have just studied. Cross out the errors and write in punctuation marks and connecting words that are needed.

The Mass to End Hunger will begin Friday evening at 7:00. We will hear about efforts to end hunger in our own city, and find out how we can help. An offering will be taken for a world hunger organization called The Hunger Project and the money will go to their work in Africa.

When the church addition is finished we will have a larger kitchen and community hall. Contact the church office if you would like to help organize our first all-congregation supper.

We have appointed Robert Malon as Sunday school director for the coming year, volunteers to teach our Sunday school classes in the fall are still needed.

Tessa Ogrodnick lost a baking pan at the brownie sale. She would like to know if anyone has found it? Call her at 445-0984

THE EDITED PIECE IS ON PAGE 156.

3. USE A COMMA AFTER AN INTRODUCTORY WORD OR PHRASE. You can tell if a word or phrase is introductory by removing it from the sentence. If the sentence that is left is a complete thought, the word or phrase is introductory.

> As a matter of fact, he's not capable of doing it.
>
> He's not capable of doing it.

You can see that *he's not capable of doing it* is a complete sentence by itself, so you know that *as a matter of fact* is an introductory phrase.

You can often identify introductory words and phrases by reading your sentence aloud. If you pause after the word or phrase at the beginning of the sentence, it may be introductory. Read the example sentence above out loud. You should have paused after *as a matter of fact.*

> Ted, is that you?
>
> In fact, I don't believe a word you said.
>
> Running to keep from getting soaked, I tripped and dropped the office mail on the wet sidewalk.

4. USE COMMAS TO SET OFF INTERRUPTING WORDS OR PHRASES. Interrupting words and phrases are similar to introductory phrases. In fact, many of the same types of words and phrases are used. Interrupting words and phrases are never part of the main idea of the sentence. If an interrupter is removed from a sentence, the sentence will remain a complete sentence. In addition, like an introductory phrase, you usually pause before and after an interrupter when you read the sentence aloud.

> I want you to know, by the way, that you are doing an excellent job.

Read the sentence above out loud. You should have paused before and after *by the way.* Now read this version of the sentence:

> I want you to know that you are doing an excellent job.

Notice that the meaning of the sentence is not changed when the phrase *by the way* is removed and that the sentence is still a complete thought.

Several common types of interrupting phrases are listed below. If you're not sure whether a word or a group of words is an interrupting phrase, check to see if it falls into one of these categories. If it doesn't, it's probably not an interrupting phrase.

Direct Address

The name of a person being spoken to is set off by commas.

I'm sick of your advice, Rob, so leave me alone.

Renaming Phrases

Some interrupting phrases describe or give information about a noun.

Seattle, my favorite city, is near both the mountains and the sea.

Melissa Peabody, the woman in the white suit, owns the company.

Extra Information

Some phrases add information that is not essential to the meaning of the sentence. Without commas to set them off, these phrases may confuse your reader.

I left, as a matter of fact, for the same reason.

You can, of course, take I-90 instead of the toll road.

The foreman, according to rumor, was replaced because he cheated the company.

Occasionally words and phrases similar to the ones above come at the end of the sentence rather than in the middle. Here are two examples:

The feud finally ended, to my surprise.

Please reconsider your decision, Mr. Romero.

5. USE COMMAS TO SEPARATE ITEMS IN A SERIES. A series is three or more items appearing one after the other. The items can be single words or phrases. Usually either *and* or *or* comes before the last item in the series.

Words

The colors we chose for the poster are yellow, purple, and red.

Her long, straight, auburn hair is silky to the touch.

Because of my new job, I will be moving to Cleveland, Dayton, or Cincinnati.

Phrases

A winning team practices, builds team spirit, and expects to win.

My boss encouraged me to work hard by paying me well, listening to my ideas, rewarding my extra efforts, and promoting me.

Don't use a comma when there are only two items.

Incorrect: Money, and power will get you ahead in life.

Correct: Money and power will get you ahead in life.

Exercise C: Editing for Punctuation

In the paragraph that follows, there are punctuation errors of all kinds. Correct them by crossing out the errors and writing in punctuation marks and joining words where necessary.

I think, that everyone ought to be allowed to have a few bad habits. How virtuous can one person be. Take my household for example. I am not a bad person but I do drink lots of beer and coffee. My husband seldom drinks beer or coffee, but, he has a habit of eating everything in sight. My mother on the other hand, will clean up the entire house but will leave stacks of magazines piled on the dining room table, the coffee table the bookshelf, the piano and any other flat surface. Even so I love living with my husband and my mother, and wouldn't want to live with perfect people.

THE EDITED PARAGRAPH IS ON PAGE 157.

6. *USE COMMAS AFTER PARTS OF ADDRESSES AND DATES.* When an address is given in a sentence, a comma should be used after the name, street address, city, and zip code but not between the state and the zip code. If only one part of an address is given, no comma is needed.

> A letter addressed to Bob Ponds, 217 Oak Terrace, Boston, MA 02134, was put in my box by mistake.
>
> Our plant in Arlington, Virginia, is being shut down.
>
> I live at 1150 N. Halsted.

In sentences, a comma is used after each number in a date if more than one number is given. A comma is also used after a day of the week if the day precedes a date. Compare the following pairs of sentences.

> She was born on October 24, 1959, in the back seat of a cab.
>
> She was born in 1959 in the back seat of a cab.
>
> On Monday, July 10, we left on our honeymoon.
>
> On July 10, 1942, we left on our honeymoon.

Now you know the most important uses of commas. Keep in mind that putting commas where they do not belong will confuse your reader just as much as leaving them out where they are needed. Unless you have a specific reason for putting in a comma, don't use one. Double-check to be sure that you are following one of the comma rules before you put a comma into a sentence.

PARAGRAPH HIGHLIGHT #7

Run-on sentences are complete thoughts strung together without punctuation or connecting words.

Run-on: I used to go to work at 8:30 now I go at 9:00.

Do you see that the two complete thoughts in the run-on sentence above run into each other? They need to be separated. Where does the second complete thought start? To repair the run-on, you need to know where the first complete thought ends (*8:30*) and the second complete thought starts (*now*).

There are three ways to repair run-on sentences. The first way is to start a new sentence where the second complete thought begins.

I used to go to work at 8:30. Now I go at 9:00.

Since the two sentences above are short and choppy, you might want to combine them into one sentence with a comma and a joining word, like this:

I used to go to work at 8:30, **but** now I go at 9:00.

The third way to repair the run-on is to insert a semicolon (;) between the two complete thoughts and add a word or phrase like *however, therefore, for example,* or *on the other hand.* These words and phrases emphasize the relationship between the two complete thoughts. You need a comma after the word or phrase that shows the relationship.

I used to go to work at 8:30; **however,** now I go at 9:00.

Paragraph Highlight Exercise 7

 Rewrite the following run-on sentences using any of the methods described above. Read each of your new sentences carefully to make sure you have chosen a good method for that run-on. Some methods will sound better than others, depending on the sentence.

1. I keep reading about how dreadful young people are these days my grandchildren are delightful.

2. Carl was caught with his hand in the cookie jar he got a spanking.

3. Mr. Fitzgerald called a meeting of all the supervisors they discussed the absentee problem.

4. I ate too much during the holidays I never want to see another Christmas cookie.

5. I went to a play last night it was about racial tensions in cities.

POSSIBLE CORRECTIONS FOR THESE RUN-ONS ARE ON PAGE 157.

Punctuating Abbreviations

There should be a period after each part of an abbreviation that stands for a word. For example, *United States of America* is abbreviated *U.S.A.*, with a period following each letter. On the other hand, the abbreviation for *Doctor*, *Dr.*, has only one period since it stands for only one word.

The most common exception to this rule is that the two-letter postal abbreviations for states (such as *CA* for *California* or *NC* for *North Carolina*) never have periods after them.

You will often see abbreviations without periods, such as FBI (Federal Bureau of Investigation) or IBM (International Business Machines). Companies and organizations sometimes decide that they prefer to abbreviate their names without periods.

titles and degrees	Mr. Don Cox, Jr. Mary Donnelly, Ph.D.
places	U.S.S.R. Ash St. Lincoln Blvd.
expressions of time	7:45 A.M. A.D. 2001 3 yrs.
dates	Aug. 12 Mon.
measurements	in. ft. mi. lb.
other	Co. Inc. Assn. etc. apt.

Mark Ester caught the train to New York, **NY,** at 3:15 **P.M.**

I hope to get a job at **St.** Mary's on Park **Ave.**

Notice that the sentences above end with abbreviations. Since the abbreviations already end with a period, you do not need to add another period at the end of the sentence.

Punctuation in Letters

There are specific rules for punctuating the parts of a letter. In the model of a business letter below, notice the commas in the addresses and the date, the colon following the greeting, and the comma following the closing. If the model were of a personal letter, a comma (instead of a colon) would be used after the greeting.

MODEL
Business Letter

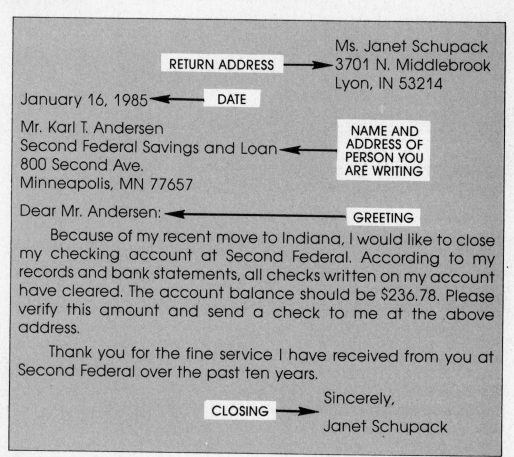

RETURN ADDRESS →

Ms. Janet Schupack
3701 N. Middlebrook
Lyon, IN 53214

January 16, 1985 ← DATE

Mr. Karl T. Andersen
Second Federal Savings and Loan ← NAME AND ADDRESS OF PERSON YOU ARE WRITING
800 Second Ave.
Minneapolis, MN 77657

Dear Mr. Andersen: ← GREETING

Because of my recent move to Indiana, I would like to close my checking account at Second Federal. According to my records and bank statements, all checks written on my account have cleared. The account balance should be $236.78. Please verify this amount and send a check to me at the above address.

Thank you for the fine service I have received from you at Second Federal over the past ten years.

CLOSING → Sincerely,

Janet Schupack

Exercise D: Editing a Personal Letter for Punctuation

In the letter that follows, there are punctuation errors of all kinds. Correct them by crossing out the errors and writing in punctuation marks that are needed. You may have to add joining words as well.

June, 12, 1985

Dear Sally;

   I know you don't love me anymore but I have to stay in touch with you. Please don't leave me out of your life. I'm not angry with you for breaking off our engagement, I just want to be friends and write once in a while.

   I really like my new job new apartment and new city. The transfer was exactly the right thing to do I think. Although I've lived here for only a short time I've gotten on my feet fast.

   I've even started dating a woman one of the four roommates who live next door. So you can see Sally I have really gotten over your leaving me.

   I want to hear about what's going on with you but I would appreciate it if you didn't tell me about any men you're involved with? Please write to me at 55 S Wellington, Champagne Hills NY 26532.

Your friend
Mike

THE EDITED LETTER IS ON PAGE 158.

Check Your Spelling

Spelling Well

Along with capitals and punctuation, spelling errors are probably the most noticeable to your reader. Misspelled words in your writing can stick out like waving red flags.

It would take you a lot of memorizing to learn to spell every word in your vocabulary. But you don't have to do that to become a good speller. If you learn a few simple rules and use a dictionary a lot, you'll spell much better.

It's hard to check your own spelling. Often you don't see things yourself that other people will see right away. The best way to check just your spelling is to go backward through your piece, looking at each word individually. That way you don't get distracted by any other aspect of the writing, and you're more likely to see spelling errors or notice words you're not sure of.

Using a Dictionary

A dictionary is the most important tool available for good spelling. You may wonder how you can look up a word in the dictionary that you can't spell. Here's how.

First, write down your best guess of how the word might be spelled. Look that spelling up in the dictionary. If that spelling isn't there, scan the page for your word.

If you didn't find it, and your word has a suffix or prefix or is a special form, look up the root word. For example, if you want to know how to spell celebration, and you can't find it, you can look up celebrate. Most dictionaries tell you how to spell different forms of root words right in the definition of the root word.

If you still haven't found the right spelling, look at your best guess spelling. Write it down again, separating the word into its different syllables so you can look at each part.

Are there any other ways that any of the sounds in these syllables could be spelled? Could any of the letters be doubled in the correct spelling? Start at the beginning of the word and think of variations for the first few letters. Write down the guesses that you think are most likely and look them up. You should be able to find the word.

For example, you might write the word *agrevate*. It doesn't look quite right to you, and you look it up in the dictionary. You can't find it in the dictionary.

Next, you write the word down in syllables, like this:

ag - re - vate

The *g* could be doubled, so you look up *aggrevate*, but that's not in the dictionary either. Next you look at *re*. The vowel sound "uh" can be spelled with almost any vowel. Now you have several good possibilities:

agruvate or aggruvate

agravate or aggravate

agrivate or aggrivate

If you start looking these up in the dictionary, you'll find that *aggravate* is the correct spelling.

This may look like a lot of work, but it will take some effort to improve your spelling. You might want to keep a list of common words that you have trouble spelling.

Look at the chart below to see letters and combinations of letters that are often exchanged for each other when a word is misspelled.

Common Spelling	Different Spelling, Same Sound
Consonants	
r, as in <u>r</u>an	<u>wr</u>ite
s, as in <u>s</u>it	<u>c</u>ity a<u>sc</u>end <u>ps</u>ycho
sh, as in <u>sh</u>oe	<u>Ch</u>evy na<u>ti</u>on discu<u>ssi</u>on
ch, as in <u>ch</u>urch	ca<u>tch</u> na<u>t</u>ure
j, as in <u>j</u>ob	dre<u>dg</u>e <u>g</u>elatin
k, as in <u>k</u>ite	<u>c</u>oma <u>ch</u>aracter ja<u>ck</u> uni<u>qu</u>e
n, as in <u>n</u>ot	<u>kn</u>ow
f, as in <u>f</u>ather	<u>ph</u>ony
Vowels	
ee, as in tr<u>ee</u>	b<u>ea</u>k secr<u>e</u>t<u>e</u> prest<u>i</u>ge ch<u>ie</u>f rec<u>ei</u>ve
a, as in arc<u>a</u>de	l<u>ai</u>d tr<u>ay</u> n<u>eigh</u>bor
o, as in st<u>o</u>ne	m<u>oa</u>n bl<u>ow</u>n
i, as in n<u>i</u>ne	p<u>ie</u> r<u>igh</u>t h<u>eigh</u>t
oo, as in n<u>oo</u>n	bl<u>ue</u> can<u>oe</u> y<u>ou</u> thr<u>ough</u> n<u>ew</u>

Continued

Continued from page 147

Combinations

er, as in read<u>er</u>	past<u>or</u>	simil<u>ar</u>
ence, as in depend<u>ence</u>	lic<u>ense</u>	avoid<u>ance</u>
ent, as in judgm<u>ent</u>	pleas<u>ant</u>	
able, as in teach<u>able</u>	terr<u>ible</u>	
le, as in app<u>le</u>	centr<u>al</u>	tins<u>el</u>
ize, as in s<u>ize</u>	fr<u>ies</u>	exerc<u>ise</u>
tion, as in na<u>tion</u>	morti<u>cian</u>	dissen<u>sion</u>

These aren't all of the possible confusing spellings of sounds. You may run across many others. In the English language there is often more than one way to spell a sound. If you can't find your word in the dictionary, think of other ways the sounds in the word could be spelled.

Exercise E: Dictionary Practice

The following words may be misspelled. Look each one up in a dictionary. If you can't find a word, use the process described above to find the correct spelling. If the spelling is incorrect, write the correct spelling in the blank. If it is correct, put a check mark in the blank.

1. relation _____
2. factory _____
3. liesure _____
4. responsible _____
5. tradicion _____
6. confidance _____
7. machine _____
8. wether _____
9. mesage _____
10. pasture _____
11. slight _____
12. ridiculus _____
13. eight _____
14. managment _____
15. axcess _____

ANSWERS ARE ON PAGE 158.

Adding Prefixes

A prefix consists of one or more letters added to the beginning of a word to change its meaning. When a prefix is added to a word, the spelling of the word itself and the spelling of the prefix <u>always</u> remain the same.

re + move = remove   over + eat = overeat

un + fit = unfit   in + complete = incomplete

Don't be confused if adding a prefix doubles the consonant. Never change the spelling of either the root word or the prefix.

il + logical = illogical   mis + spelled = misspelled

Another error you might make is doubling a consonant when you add a prefix.

Incorrect: dis + appear = dissappear

Correct: dis + appear = disappear

Adding Suffixes

A suffix consists of one or more letters added to the end of a word to change its meaning. Usually when you add a suffix to the end of a word, the spelling of the word and the spelling of the suffix remain the same.

final + ly =   smooth + ness =
  finally   smoothness

However, there are some exceptions.

1. If a root word ends with a silent *e*, and the suffix begins with a vowel, you should drop the *e* when you add a suffix.

please + ing = pleasing   dance + ed = danced

But if there is a soft *g* (as in *gesture*) or a soft *c* (as in *city*) before the silent *e*, and you are adding *able* or *ous*, you have to keep the *e* to show that the sound is soft.

courage + ous =   notice + able =
  courag<u>e</u>ous   notic<u>e</u>able

2. If the root word ends in *y* preceded by a consonant, the *y* becomes *i* when you add a suffix.

happy + ness =   angry + ly =
  happ<u>i</u>ness   angr<u>i</u>ly

However, if the suffix you're adding begins with *i*, the root word does not change because then there would be two *i*'s in a row.

carry + ing = carrying

3. Sometimes the final consonant of a root word has to be doubled when you add a suffix. In this case, the following three things have to be true:

a. The stress must be on the last (or only) syllable of the root word. For example, the stress is on the last syllable of the word *regret*. When you pronounce it, you say "re-GRET," not "RE-gret."

b. The root word has to end with a single consonant other than *h*, *w*, or *x*, preceded by a single vowel.

c. The suffix has to start with a vowel.

stop + ing = sto<u>pp</u>ing   occur + ence = occu<u>rr</u>ence

According to this rule, if you add the suffix *ed* to the word *review*, do you have to double the final consonant? Look at each of the three parts of the rule. (a) The stress is on the final syllable. You pronounce it "re-VIEW." (b) The root word ends with a single consonant preceded by a single vowel, but it is a *w*. Now you know not to double the final consonant.

review + ed = reviewed

Exercise F: Adding Prefixes and Suffixes

Add the prefix or suffix and fill in the blanks with the correct spelling.

1. agree + able = _____

2. mistake + en = _____

3. un + natural = _____

4. fly + ing = _____

5. forget + ing = _____

6. dis + associate = _____

7. lucky + er = _____

8. trace + able = _____

ANSWERS ARE ON PAGE 159.

Confusing Soundalike Words

There are some words that are often confused because they either sound exactly alike or very similar. Making mistakes with these words can create lots of confusion for your reader. Study the meanings and spellings of the following confusing sets of words.

already (previously)	I had already left.
all ready (entirely ready)	Go when you're all ready.
all right	Don't worry, things will be all right. (There is no word alright.)
altogether (entirely)	She's altogether too rude.
all together (in one place)	I have the parts all together.
capital (city or major)	Murder is a capital offense.
capitol (building)	The state capitol is white.
its (possessive)	The dog chased its tail.
it's (it is)	It's raining.
lead (go first)	Lead the way.
led (went first)	No, I led before.
lead (metal)	The pipe is made of lead.
passed (verb)	I passed a truck.
past (time or place)	I drove past it often in the past.
personal (of a certain person)	He has personal goals.
personnel (employees)	The office personnel left.
principal (school head, or main one)	The principal was the principal speaker.
principle (law or ethic)	She has high principles.
there (location or existence)	There are three eggs.
their (possessive)	Their car is a Ford.
they're (they are)	They're moving soon.
to (part of an infinitive, or a preposition)	He's going to go to town.
too (also or excessively)	He too is too late.
two (one plus one)	Two men loved her.
who's (who is or who has)	Who's talking?
whose (possessive)	Whose car is that?
your (possessive)	Your lunch is here.
you're (you are)	You're a carpenter?

Exercise G: Editing for Spelling Errors

The following piece contains nineteen misspellings. Not all are misspellings of the particular types you've just studied. Look at each word in the piece carefully. Remember that a good way to check for spelling is to go backward through the piece, word by word. Use the dictionary to look up any word you're not sure of. Cross out the misspelled words and write in the correct spellings. Then check through the piece again to be sure that you have the right nineteen words.

When my youngest bruther started first grade, my mother also returned to sckool. It was tougf for us because we were used to haveing her at home. Now she was frequently abscent. She woud close herself up in her room to study, to. We found it extremly frustrating when she was home but wouldn't talk too us. Their were times when we felt desserted. However, we became acustomed to her bing in shcool, and eventualy she went to work. Loooking back, I see that we grew a lot and learned to take responsability for ourselfs in those days. I think my brothers and I are better addults because we had a working mother.

CORRECTIONS ARE ON PAGE 159.

Exercise H: Editing tor Capitalization, Punctuation, and Spelling

Part 1

There are all types of errors in the following letter. Cross out the mistakes and write in corrections.

James E Finley

592 E. 5th Street.

Carson, KS, 63097

September, 1, 1985

Jeannine Hamler

Director of Public Relations

KROI Radio

24, Brower St.

Carson, KS 63095

Dear Ms Hamler,

I am riting to ask your radio station to record, and play a public servise announcment for a benefit costume ball on halloween. All profets will go to the Carson Children's Services Center. The center provides services for Physically, and Mentally handicaped children in the Carson area.

Because the purpose of the dance is to raise money, we are asking local orgenizations like KROI Radio to donate goods and services. Our goal is to raise $10,000. We already have promises from two Dance bands to play for free. Hemingway's a Department store, will be donateing prizes for six costume catigories the Carson association of Restaurants and Hotels is arranging all food and drink sales. Won't you join them in supporting the Children's Services Center.

Continued

The Carson Halloween Ball will be held at the Carson civic coliseum on Thursday October 1 at 7:00 P.M. It will be a famly and comunity event, and people of all ages will be welcome. The first band will be Country Joe Shuffletoe, a country-Western band. The second band will be Peggy's Pursuit a faverite Rock band.

I hope, to here from you in the coming week to make arrangements for publicity throw KROI radio. Thank you for you're time and consideration.

Sincerely;

James Finley
Dance Committee

THE EDITED LETTER IS ON PAGE 160.

Part 2

Return to a piece of writing of your own from Chapter 3, 4, or 5. Edit it for spelling, capitalization, and punctuation. Also make any other improvements you can in grammar and word choice.

Preparing Final Copy

You have learned a great deal about the writing process. You have brainstormed, outlined, written a first draft, revised, fine-tuned your word choice, and edited. All that remains is preparing and proofreading final copy.

Before you write out the final copy of a piece of writing, choose the kind of paper that's right for the job. You might use personal stationery, company letterhead, or plain typing paper. Then either write or type as neatly as you can. Be sure to indent each paragraph and write on every line. If you are using a special form, like a memo or letter, be sure you get all the special parts right.

Proofread your final copy. Proofreading is simply reading your piece one last time to be sure that everything is right. Sometimes, in the process of recopying, new mistakes are made by accident. So you need to check everything. Make sure all the paragraphs and sentences are complete and in order. Make sure no words have been left out. Be sure grammar, capitals, punctuation, and spelling are correct. Check your page numbers, titles, headings, and any other special features.

You should proofread at a time when you are really able to concentrate. In addition, you should try to put your piece aside for a day or so before you proofread it. It is even better if you can have someone else proofread after you finish.

In the next exercise you will have a chance to prepare a final copy.

Exercise I: Preparing Final Copy

Return to the piece that you edited in Exercise H, Part 2, on page 154. Prepare final copy for your piece. Be sure to proofread it carefully and make it neat.

Answers

Exercise A

Super Ḃowl Ṣunday has got to be the most controversial event of the year in my family. You'd think my children were the Ḟootball Ṗlayers. My Ṣon and daughter always have to choose opposite sides. When the Miami Ḋolphins played the San Francisco 49ers, they argued for days about which Ṭeam should win. They even wrote an article for their high school paper, "Brother Ȧnd Sister Ḋivide Family on Super Bowl Question." They interviewed their Ġrandfather in Miami and their Ȧunt Sarah in Ṣan Francisco by phone for the article.

Exercise B

The Mass to End Hunger will begin Friday evening at 7:00. We will hear about efforts to end hunger in our own city͵ and find out how we can help. An offering will be taken for a world hunger organization called The Hunger Project͵ and the money will go to their work in Africa.

When the church addition is finished͵ we will have a larger kitchen and community hall. Contact the church office if you would like to help organize our first all-congregation supper.

We have appointed Robert Malon as Sunday school director for the coming year͵ Ṿolunteers to teach our Sunday school classes in the fall are still needed.

Tessa Ogrodnick lost a baking pan at the brownie sale. She would like to know if anyone has found it͵ Call her at 445-0984͵

Exercise C

I think, that everyone ought to be allowed to have a few bad habits. How virtuous can one person be? Take my household, for example. I am not a bad person, but I do drink lots of beer and coffee. My husband seldom drinks beer or coffee, but, he has a habit of eating everything in sight. My mother, on the other hand, will clean up the entire house but will leave stacks of magazines piled on the dining room table, the coffee table, the bookshelf, the piano, and any other flat surface. Even so, I love living with my husband and my mother, and wouldn't want to live with perfect people.

Paragraph Highlight Exercise 7

These sentences could be repaired in several different ways. If your sentences are different from the ones below, read each of your sentences to yourself. How do they sound? Look at the models again. Is your punctuation correct? If you added words, do they make sense in the sentences? Do the words you added fit the punctuation?

1. I keep reading about how dreadful young people are these days; **however,** my grandchildren are delightful.
2. Carl was caught with his hand in the cookie jar, **so** he got a spanking.
3. Mr. Fitzgerald called a meeting of all the supervisors. They discussed the absentee problem.
4. I ate too much during the holidays; **in fact,** I never want to see another Christmas cookie.
5. I went to a play last night. It was about racial tensions in cities.

Exercise D

June 12, 1985

Dear Sally

I know you don't love me anymore, but I have to stay in touch with you. Please don't leave me out of your life. I'm not angry with you for breaking off our engagement, I just want to be friends and write once in a while.

I really like my new job, new apartment, and new city. The transfer was exactly the right thing to do, I think. Although I've lived here for only a short time, I've gotten on my feet fast.

I've even started dating a woman, one of the four roommates who live next door. So you can see, Sally, I have really gotten over your leaving me.

I want to hear about what's going on with you, but I would appreciate it if you didn't tell me about any men you're involved with. Please write to me at 55 S. Wellington, Champagne Hills NY 26532.

Your friend,

Mike

Exercise E

1. relation   ✓
2. factory   ✓
3. liesure   **leisure**
4. responsible   ✓
5. tradicion   **tradition**
6. confidance   **confidence**
7. machine   ✓
8. wether   **whether** or **weather**

9. mesage   **message**
10. pasture   ✓
11. slight   ✓
12. ridiculus   **ridiculous**
13. eight   ✓
14. managment   **management**
15. axcess   **access** or **excess**

Exercise F

1. agree + able = **agreeable**
2. mistake + en = **mistaken**
3. un + natural = **unnatural**
4. fly + ing = **flying**

5. forget + ing = **forgetting**
6. dis + associate = **disassociate**
7. lucky + er = **luckier**
8. trace + able = **traceable**

Exercise G

When my youngest ~~bruther~~ *brother* started first grade, my mother also returned to ~~sekool~~ *school*. It was ~~tougf~~ *tough* for us because we were used to ~~haveing~~ *having* her at home. Now she was frequently ~~abscent~~ *absent*. She ~~woud~~ *would* close herself up in her room to study, ~~to~~ *too*. We found it ~~extremly~~ *extremely* frustrating when she was home but wouldn't talk ~~too~~ *to* us. ~~Their~~ *There* were times when we felt ~~desserted~~ *deserted*. However, we became ~~acustomed~~ *accustomed* to her ~~bing~~ *being* in ~~sheool~~ *school*, and ~~eventualy~~ *eventually* she went to work. ~~Loolking~~ *Looking* back, I see that we grew a lot and learned to take ~~responsability~~ *responsibility* for ~~ourselfs~~ *ourselves* in those days. I think my brothers and I are better ~~addults~~ *adults* because we had a working mother.

Exercise H

Part 1

James E. Finley

592 E. 5th Street

Carson, KS. 63097

September 1, 1985

Jeannine Hamler

Director of Public Relations

KROI Radio

24 Brower St.

Carson, KS 63095

Dear Ms Hamler

     writing
I am ~~riting~~ to ask your radio station to record and play a public
service announcement
~~servise announcement~~ for a benefit costume ball on Halloween. All
profits
~~profets~~ will go to the Carson Children's Services Center. The center
    P   m   *handicapped*
provides services for Physically and Mentally ~~handicaped~~ children in
the Carson area.

    Because the purpose of the dance is to raise money, we are
      organizations
asking local ~~orgenizations~~ like KROI Radio to donate goods and
services. Our goal is to raise $10,000. We already have promises from
   d
two Dance bands to play for free. Hemingway's a Department store,
    donating   *categories* T   A
will be ~~donateing~~ prizes for six costume ~~catigories~~ the Carson association
of Restaurants and Hotels is arranging all food and drink sales.
Won't you join them in supporting the Children's Services Center?

The Carson Halloween Ball will be held at the Carson Çivic [C] Çoliseum on Thursday, October 1 at 7:00 P.M. It will be a family [family] and comunity [community] event, and people of all ages will be welcome. The first band will be Country Joe Shuffletoe, a country-Western [w] band. The second band will be Peggy's Pursuit, a faverite [favorite] Rock [r] band.

I hope to here [hear] from you in the coming week to make arrangements for publicity throw [through] KROI radio. Thank you for you're [your] time and consideration.

Sincerely,
James Finley
James Finley

Dance Committee

9. Using Models

How to Use This Chapter

This chapter gives you models of many different pieces of writing. Use each model as a guide as you do the exercise that follows it. Remember, your piece of writing does not have to look exactly like the model, but it should have all the important features that are pointed out to you.

Personal Writing

Organization Bulletin

If you belong to a club, church group, or any other community organization, you may need to write a notice or bulletin about past or upcoming events. Parts of the bulletin will be informative, and other parts may be narrative or persuasive. Notice how the bulletin below gives specific information when needed and how all ideas are presented in logical order.

DATE AND ORGANIZATION TITLES

> ### St. Agnes Bulletin
>
> Date: August 23, 1985
>
> To: All parish members
>
> From: Church Committee
>
> #### Recent Events:
>
> The annual parish auction was last Saturday, and over 150 people attended. Furniture, clothing, and gift certificates were sold, and the proceeds came to $1,400. We wish to thank Mr.

and Mrs. Sheehan for their help in organizing this successful event.

On August 19, the family supper was held in the church basement, and thanks go to Father Calhoun for serving as chief cook.

Upcoming Events:

Please remember that next Sunday marks the fifteenth anniversary of St. Agnes Church, and a special collection will be held to help offset the church debt. We hope that we all will be as generous as possible.

Funeral services for Mr. Pedro Rodriguez will be held on Saturday, August 24.

Reminders:

Please note that all entries for the weekly church bulletin must be received no later than the Thursday prior to each printing. Entries that do not meet this deadline will not appear in the bulletin.

LATEST
NEWS WITH
SPECIFIC NAMES
AND DATES

Exercise A: Writing a Bulletin

If you belong to a club or community organization, write a bulletin like the model above that tells of past and future events or anything else you would like to include for your readers. Make sure it has the important features that have been pointed out for you. If you do not actually belong to this kind of organization, make up a temple, church, community organization, or club bulletin for practice.

Diary or Journal Entry

A diary or journal is a place where you can write down the events of a day—what happened to you, what your feelings were, or what you learned. Sometimes a writer can use a diary to record personal things that only she will ever read. Other times, a journal is meant for others to read. As the writer, you make the choice.

The model below shows you some of the important elements of a journal entry. This writer chose to use the journal as a way to organize his life and record personal thoughts.

DATE AND TIME OF WRITING ENTRY	Date: July 29, 1985 Time: 10:00 P.M.
OVERVIEW OF DAY	Today was a better day than I thought it would be. The math test I had to take was pretty easy, and work seemed to go by quickly.
SPECIFIC GOALS DISCUSSED	The main things I wanted to accomplish today had to be put off until later. As I wrote yesterday, I wanted to ask my boss for more responsibility, and I wanted to start working on painting the kitchen. First of all, my boss was in a really bad mood today, so I thought I should wait until she cooled down before I talked with her. Second, by the time I got home from the math test, I was too tired to think about painting. I had a beer and read some magazines instead.
SUMMARY THOUGHTS	Overall, I still feel organized and in control of my life. Even though I had to put a couple of things off, I did it for good reasons, not just because I felt lazy.

Exercise B: Writing a Journal or Diary Entry

 Write a diary or journal entry about yesterday. You may want to record personal thoughts and goals, as the writer above did. Or, you may want to use the space just to record the events that took place in your life. You may want to focus on work, or school, or family life, or you may want to just mention some important events from all of these areas. Also, you may write either for yourself or for someone else.

Letter of Sympathy

When something bad happens to someone you know, it is often difficult to find the right words to tell that person you care. Remember that there is no one "right thing" to say in these situations. The best thing you can do is to be yourself when you write. If it is not your normal style, writing long, flowery, and wordy letters can seem phony. Try to write briefly and to the point because this is the best way to get across your message of caring.

The model below was written to someone whose father was in an accident. Sympathy letters can be written for many different reasons, and this is just one of them. Notice that the writer does not ramble on and on; instead, she shows her concern in short, concise paragraphs.

February 9, 1987 ◄———— DATE

Dear Geraldine, ◄———— INFORMAL GREETING

    I was sorry to hear about your father's accident. Please let him know that all of us are thinking about him and wish him well. We all miss his jokes and cheery smile.

    If there is anything that I can do for you during this difficult time, Geraldine, please let me know. Keep in touch.

                 With love,

                 Ladonna

EXPRESSES
CONCERN
UP FRONT

OFFERS
HELP

CLOSING

SIGNATURE

Exercise C: Writing a Sympathy Note

 A sympathy letter can be written when someone dies or is ill or when someone you know is feeling down about something. For this exercise, write a sympathy letter for a real or made-up situation. Remember to be yourself and to make the letter short and concise.

Letter of Request

Have you ever needed to request something in writing? For example, have you ever wanted to set up a meeting with a counselor or schoolteacher? Or have you ever wanted a store to send you its catalogue? These occasions call for letters of request. The most important thing to remember about this kind of writing is to state clearly what you want from your reader.

Notice that in the model below the important features of a request letter are pointed out for you.

                        18 Balsam Circle
RETURN ADDRESS ———►Reading, MA 01867
    TODAY'S DATE ———►August 2, 1986

Dear Mr. Tyburk, ◄———— GREETING

    My son, Alfred Canedo, is a seventh grade student at Parker Junior High. His teachers have told me that if I want to discuss his learning disability I should contact you, the guidance counselor.

    Is it possible to set up an appointment to talk to you, Mr. Tyburk? I am concerned that Alfred will not be able to do the work required for final exams, and I would like to know if he will be promoted to eighth grade if he does not pass all of them.

Continued

GIVES SPECIFIC
AND NECESSARY
FACTS

CLEARLY STATES
REASON FOR
WRITING

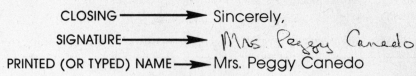

GIVES PHONE
NUMBER

Continued from page 165

I can be reached all day at 944-0822. Please call me so that we can arrange a day and time. Thank you for your help, Mr. Tyburk.

CLOSING ⟶ Sincerely,

SIGNATURE ⟶ *Mrs. Peggy Canedo*

PRINTED (OR TYPED) NAME ⟶ Mrs. Peggy Canedo

Exercise D: Writing a Request Letter

Think of something that you want or need from a person or company or organization. Write a letter to request it. Your request can be for anything from an appointment to a new set of instructions for your washing machine. Remember to say up front and clearly what you would like from your reader.

Letter to the Editor

In most newspapers and magazines, there is a special page where letters from readers appear. These letters may represent readers' opinions on articles that appeared in that publication. Or they may be opinions on a wide variety of issues in society. Look at the model of a letter to the editor below. Notice how the opinion is stated clearly and supported.

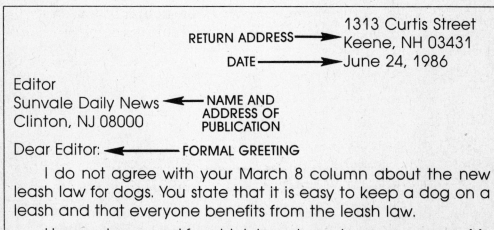

RETURN ADDRESS ⟶ 1313 Curtis Street
Keene, NH 03431

DATE ⟶ June 24, 1986

Editor
Sunvale Daily News ⟵ NAME AND ADDRESS OF PUBLICATION
Clinton, NJ 08000

Dear Editor: ⟵ FORMAL GREETING

GIVES SPECIFIC
INFORMATION
AND STATES
OPINION CLEARLY

I do not agree with your March 8 column about the new leash law for dogs. You state that it is easy to keep a dog on a leash and that everyone benefits from the leash law.

I have a large yard for which I pay huge taxes every year. My dog has been well trained for years to stay on our property. She very rarely wanders onto the sidewalk or street. Why should I have to put her on a leash?

No one in my neighborhood benefits when I put Tammy on a leash. She barks all day and night long—something that I'm sure is more annoying than seeing her step onto the street once in a while.

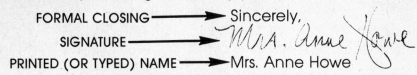

If well-behaved dogs like Tammy must be put on leashes, we should also consider putting leashes on some of those unruly kids who are always cutting across my yard.

FORMAL CLOSING ⟶ Sincerely,

SIGNATURE ⟶ *Mrs. Anne Howe*

PRINTED (OR TYPED) NAME ⟶ Mrs. Anne Howe

Exercise E: Writing a Letter to the Editor

Think of a topic you have a strong opinion about. It can be anything from police brutality to why the Dallas Cowboys lost a football game. Often you can get ideas to write about from reading your local newspaper and forming an opinion about an article. Once you have decided on a topic and your opinion on the topic, write a letter to the editor of a newspaper or magazine. Use the model above to refresh your memory on what should be included in a good letter to the editor.

Business Writing

Letter of Application

Whether you are applying to a school program or applying for a job, you'll want your application letter to be professional and well written. This is often one of the most important things you write since it can create a first impression for an employer or school director. In the model below, pay particular attention to the features pointed out to you. The same features apply to a job application letter as well.

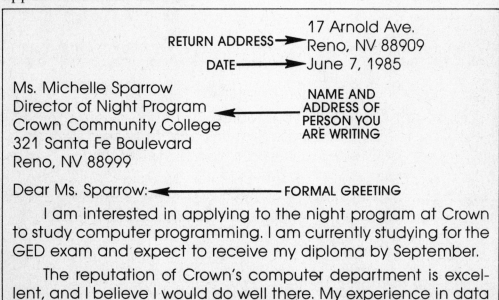

RETURN ADDRESS ⟶ 17 Arnold Ave.
Reno, NV 88909

DATE ⟶ June 7, 1985

Ms. Michelle Sparrow
Director of Night Program ⟵ NAME AND ADDRESS OF PERSON YOU ARE WRITING
Crown Community College
321 Santa Fe Boulevard
Reno, NV 88999

Dear Ms. Sparrow: ⟵ FORMAL GREETING

I am interested in applying to the night program at Crown to study computer programming. I am currently studying for the GED exam and expect to receive my diploma by September.　STATES PURPOSE UP FRONT

The reputation of Crown's computer department is excellent, and I believe I would do well there. My experience in data　BRIEFLY DESCRIBES BACKGROUND

Continued

Continued from page 167

processing and the electronics field has shown me that a career in computers would be a wise choice.

REQUESTS APPOINTMENT

Is it possible for me to come in for an interview, Ms. Sparrow? I will be happy to provide you with any other information you need about me and my qualifications. Thank you for your time.

FORMAL CLOSING ⟶ Sincerely,

SIGNATURE ⟶ *Jonathan K. Milley*

PRINTED (OR TYPED) NAME ⟶ Jonathan K. Milley

Exercise F: Writing an Application Letter

If you are applying to a school or for a job, this is the perfect opportunity to put your application letter in writing. If you are not in one of these situations, write an application letter anyway. This will be good practice for when you actually need to write such a letter. Use the model above to guide you.

Job Memo

You may sometimes need or be asked to write a memo about a procedure or event that took place on the job. A memo is different from a letter or report because it is usually shorter and more direct than these other kinds of writing. A job memo is meant to convey information in as efficient a manner as possible. Things like irrelevant ideas and personal comments are generally frowned upon in a job situation. The model job memo below shows you the important features of this kind of writing.

TODAY'S DATE

May 15, 1985

To: Steve Kiernan / Print Supplies ⟵ NAME AND DEPARTMENT OF PERSON YOU ARE WRITING

From: Joanna Schwartz / Floor 3 ⟵ YOUR NAME AND DEPARTMENT

SUBJECT OF MEMO

Re: Ink supplies shortage

GIVES SPECIFIC REASON FOR MEMO

As we discussed Monday, May 13, this memo will serve as a reminder about the new procedures for ink shortages. Please post this notice for all employees.

PRESENTS IMPORTANT FACTS WITHOUT PERSONAL COMMENTS

When print ink supplies are below one-quarter of usual stock, your office will alert the on-duty supervisor on Floor 3. The supervisor will then check remaining job requests and order additional ink from the warehouse if necessary. Your department should be prepared for delivery at all times.

This new procedure should help prevent line shutdowns as well as excess stock. Please let me know if there is any problem with this system.

Exercise G: Writing a Job Memo

 Imagine that you work in an office supply shop. You are planning to be out of town Tuesday and Wednesday next week. You would like to tell your supervisor, April Moore, that a co-worker, Kathleen Mealey, will take care of setting up your displays. In addition, Reed Ingersell will take your register shift.

Put this information into a job memo format. Use the model above to help you and remember to include all relevant and specific information.

Resumé

A **resumé** is an organized way of presenting your qualifications to a potential employer. Rather than writing four or five paragraphs describing yourself, you can use this format to clearly present facts about your experience.

The model below indicates the features of a good resumé. Notice how only important experiences and qualifications are listed. Although you may have held a wider variety of jobs, try to choose only those that will be considered important to an employer.

	Michael Simon 400 Jamaica Way Boston, MA 01867 (617) 555-9181	YOUR NAME, ADDRESS, AND TELEPHONE NUMBER
Job Interests	—any entry-level position in the field of hotel or motel management	WHAT POSITION YOU ARE LOOKING FOR
Job Experience	—(May 1985–May 1986) Desk Clerk Holiday Inn, Inc. 491 East Park Duluth, MN 61113 —(February 1984–May 1985) Receptionist Keenan Catering Service Montvale Plaza Duluth, MN 61111	WHAT JOB EXPERIENCE YOU HAVE HAD
Education	—1985; completed one year toward Associate's Degree Barton County Community College Duluth, MN 61115 —1984; graduated from Farmington High School Farmington, MN 62121	WHAT EDUCATIONAL BACKGROUND YOU HAVE

Exercise H: Writing a Resumé

Take this opportunity to write your own resumé. Include all the features from the model above and be specific with all information.

Cover Letter

If you want to send your resumé to a particular company or organization, you will probably want to enclose a cover letter with it. A **cover letter** can state your interest in a certain position in the company, or it can just introduce you to the reader. The cover letter can also emphasize key points in your resumé or include any information that has been left off the resumé.

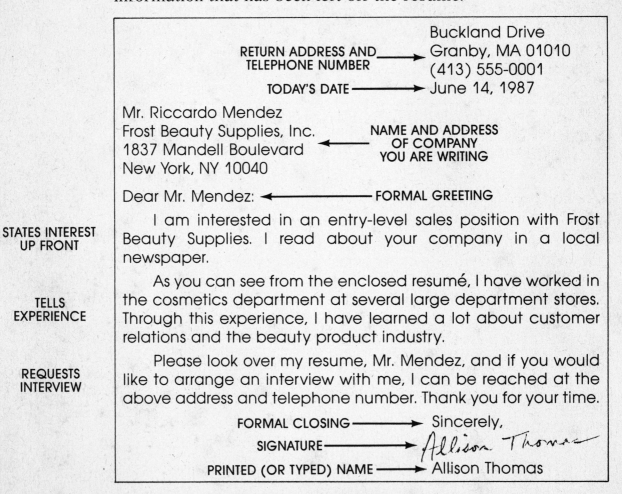

RETURN ADDRESS AND TELEPHONE NUMBER → Buckland Drive / Granby, MA 01010 / (413) 555-0001

TODAY'S DATE → June 14, 1987

Mr. Riccardo Mendez
Frost Beauty Supplies, Inc.
1837 Mandell Boulevard
New York, NY 10040
← NAME AND ADDRESS OF COMPANY YOU ARE WRITING

Dear Mr. Mendez: ← FORMAL GREETING

STATES INTEREST UP FRONT

I am interested in an entry-level sales position with Frost Beauty Supplies. I read about your company in a local newspaper.

TELLS EXPERIENCE

As you can see from the enclosed resumé, I have worked in the cosmetics department at several large department stores. Through this experience, I have learned a lot about customer relations and the beauty product industry.

REQUESTS INTERVIEW

Please look over my resume, Mr. Mendez, and if you would like to arrange an interview with me, I can be reached at the above address and telephone number. Thank you for your time.

FORMAL CLOSING → Sincerely,

SIGNATURE → *Allison Thomas*

PRINTED (OR TYPED) NAME → Allison Thomas

Exercise I: Writing a Cover Letter

Now write a cover letter to accompany the resumé you wrote in Exercise H. If you do not actually want to send out a resumé at this time, make up a company name and practice writing to the personnel department there. Use the model above to guide you.